Do We Have To Work?

The Big Idea
Matthew Taylor

Do We Have To Work?

A primer for the 21st century

Over 190 illustrations

Contents

Introduction

A

Most of us must work. We divide our lives into work and leisure. Work is where we derive our status and a sense of purpose, not to mention a way of paying our bills. The role of work is a major issue in all cultures, belief systems and political movements. Campaigners have argued for less work, fairer work, control over work, meaningful work, jobs for all and an end to wage slavery.

We have internalized beliefs about the value of work and built our economies and lives around those beliefs. Work is so much part of our lives and our culture we can forget how the prevalence of paid employment is a relatively recent phenomenon. Now, a combination of technology, economics and environmental necessity is creating the possibility of working less and working better.

In all societies the way we think about and undertake work reflects, and often reinforces, power relations and the ideology that supports those relations. Not only the division of labour but the definition of work – including the devaluing of caring – is central to the feminist critique of patriarchy. The ideology and bogus science of racism grew up in part to justify an exploitative form of labour relation: slavery. Although categories of social class have become more complex and arguably less likely to determine attitudes and affiliations than in the past, the division between the owners and managers of capital and those who must work for them is still a fundamental part of our political economy. A critique of the nature of work and the articulation of an alternative world of good work is part of most visions of social transformation.

A   Commuters on their way to work in the City of London during the morning rush hour, and on their way home at the end of the working day, walking over London Bridge. One of the many sights that disappeared during the COVID-19 lockdown.
B   Alternative communities, such as this commune in Wales, often include ways of working that are entirely collective, or reject the use of modern technology.

Patriarchy is when the father or eldest male is head of the family, and descent is through the male line. It also has the wider meaning of a society run by, and for, men.

The most basic question, of whether we need to work at all, appears to have several affirmative answers. Our standard of living relies on a complex labour market in which many people must perform functions necessary for the economic and social system to function. It seems inevitable that a lot of this work will be undertaken, not because people choose it as a lifestyle or a route to fulfilment, but primarily because they get paid to do it.

Equally, because almost no one chooses the life of a hermit, we will create unpaid work as a by-product of what we want from life. While the people of poor countries often have to shoulder exhausting and dangerous work to survive, middle class citizens of the rich world have replaced the largely physical burdens of subsistence with the psychological burdens of modern living.

A

Labour market describes the relationship between the supply of people wanting to work and the demand to hire workers. A tight labour market is one with low unemployment.

A   Migrant workers earn a basic living performing hard physical work in harsh conditions in a brick kiln in Bhaktapur, Nepal. Much work around the world continues to be exhausting and dangerous.

B   Commuters stand packed in an overcrowded bus, traversing downtown Yangon, Myanmar. The daily commute has become an integral part of our idea of regular, salaried, office work.

Yet, if the purpose of life is to achieve some sense of fulfilment, arguably the form of work we seem collectively least able to generate is the form we most deeply need. Most people express satisfaction with their paid employment. But, according to Gallup, the global polling company and consultancy that advises many employers, only a small minority say they are fully engaged at work. Equally, while around three quarters of people in the UK report good levels of wellbeing, how many of us can say we are truly able to fulfil our potential?

A

In the wake of the coronavirus pandemic, many of us have had to change our working patterns. The question of how best to balance work and the rest of life was an issue before the COVID crisis, with a growth in forms of working which offer flexibility in terms of hours and location. The pros and cons of working from home during the pandemic have led both individuals and organizations to think more deeply about how the balance between work and the rest of our lives could change. People were pleased to stop commuting but many missed spending time face to face with colleagues. While flexibility for more secure and better paid workers can be reciprocal, benefitting employers and employees, at the lower end of the labour market, flexibility for bosses often means precariousness for workers. The pandemic raised public awareness of the poor terms and conditions suffered by many key workers, whether social care assistants or parcel couriers.

The issues raised by COVID are broader than work. Crises do not always lead to fundamental change, nor is change always for the good. But the reasons to re-imagine the future existed before anyone had heard of COVID-19. High levels of inequality, anger and polarization in many developed societies had undermined faith in progress.

The liberal democratic system which only a generation ago seemed globally triumphant is now attacked from all sides, its survival dependent on achieving a level of unity and a scale of reform of which it currently seems incapable. Added to this are two factors bound to change our worlds.

First the existential crisis of climate change. It is difficult to see how the human race can head off the worst impact of global warming without major and rapid changes in our economies, aspirations and lifestyles.

A   Enforced working from home during the COVID-19 pandemic prompted widespread discussion of its pros and cons among both employers and employees.

B   A normally bustling Piccadilly Circus, London, is deserted during lockdown in the UK, April 2020.

C   A Deliveroo courier, wearing a protective mask, cycles through Paris, France, April 2020. These low-paid workers, often lacking employment rights, were proved essential during lockdown.

Liberal democratic system generally refers to societies that combine democratic safeguards, civil liberties and open but regulated markets with a base line of social protections for citizens.

Second, the impact of widespread and profound technological change. The goal of technology is surely to make life better, yet there is concern and anger about its current effects on our lives and fear about the even greater impact it could have in the future. An RSA survey in 2018 found workers were four times as likely to think technology would reduce control and autonomy at work as increase it. When it comes to work, rather than being empowered by technology, we are more often portrayed as the hapless victims of inexorable change.

A   Workers sit in front of their computer screens at two call centres in the Philippines. Information technology has made a huge impact on work, but many employees are pessimistic about future change.

B   Changes in employment conditions can lead to organization and oppostion. Here, feminist protesters march through Paris, France, in boiler suits, during a day of protest and ongoing transport worker strikes over French pension reform plans; January 2020.

A

B

At a time of public pessimism, when we seem to have lost faith in the possibility of human progress and development, good work for all could be a rallying cry. It is an aim that would require radical change not just to work but to the society that generates it. To be able to imagine such a future we need to explore what we mean by work, the way our working lives have changed across human history, why work so often feels onerous and oppressive, and what might turn work from something many people feel forced to do into to something we all enthusiastically choose.

1. What Is Work and Why Do We Do It?

A

Hannah Arendt was a German-born American political philosopher. Her writings on political theory and philosophy made her one of the most important political thinkers of the 20th century.

Utopia – literally from the Greek 'no' and 'place' – was coined by philosopher, author and statesman Sir Thomas More (1478–1535) as the title for his satirical novel about a fictional island society.

For most adults below retirement age, the question 'What work do you do?' is straightforward. The answer relates to our primary paid occupation. It might be a job that has existed for centuries, a teacher or doctor or farmer, or perhaps an occupation that has grown in recent years; a software designer, a management consultant, a barista. Alternatively, we might refer to our employment status, 'I run my own business', 'I'm an actor but I drive taxis to pay the bills', 'I'm a hairdresser on maternity leave'. Sadly, right now, the answer for too many is 'I am unemployed'.

But a job is not the only work we do. Many thinkers have identified different categories of human activity. The philosopher Hannah Arendt (1906–75) distinguished between 'labour', which is necessary for subsistence and reproduction, 'work' which is about changing the world around us to meet our needs and 'action' which concerns the way in which each person exists as a free individual in society. Along similar lines, we can think about the role of work in our lives as a spectrum of motivation. At the extrinsic end is paid employment, which we tend to think of as something we do in order to earn money and so we can enjoy the rest of our lives. At the other, intrinsic, end is the idea of a 'life's work', motivated by the desire for self-expression, purpose and fulfilment. Between the two is the necessary but unpaid work generated by simply living the lives we choose in the circumstances in which we find ourselves.

Throughout history utopian visions have envisaged a society in which almost all forms of onerous effort are unnecessary. Perhaps to provide escapism from the poverty and oppression of daily existence, a popular medieval myth was Cockaigne, a land in which people could not only lead lives of luxury, or even debauchery, but where, according to historian Herman Pleij, 'roasted pigs wander about with knives in their back to make carving easy, where geese fly directly into one's mouth, where cooked fish jump out of the water and land at one's feet'.

B

A   Three calendar images – March, June and October – from the *Très Riches Heures du Duc de Berry*, created between 1412 and 1416 by the Limbourg brothers. They depict peasants performing agricultural work appropriate to each month, against a background of remarkable medieval architecture.

B   The mythical work-free land of Cockaigne was a popular idea in medieval Europe. In this coloured engraving some people ride horses and boar, while others play musical instruments.

A The owners of capital have often been seen as living a life of leisure on the backs of working people. This 1883 political cartoon by Puck, entitled 'The protectors of our industries', depicts low-wage workers, bent over with the strain, holding up a raft carrying rich industrialists with bellies full of dollars.

B The affluent post-war home featured a range of labour-saving products. While many feel that technology makes life more complicated, adverts, such as this one from 1946 for a Maytag washing machine, promise new products will make life easier and reduce unnecessary work.

As Andrea Komlosy explains in her book *Work: The Last 1,000 Years,* the meaning attached to terms for work tends to narrow as paid employment becomes the norm. Dating back to the ancient Greek word '*ponos*' (to toil or exert oneself), the idea of work has included all effortful and onerous activities. For poor people in poor societies the day-to-day work of survival can be massively onerous. The lives of the those who lack access to safe drinking water and have to travel sometimes miles to obtain it (80% of such water fetching is done by women) would be transformed if all they had to do was turn a tap in their kitchen. Reducing unnecessary human effort, especially in relation to tasks vital to survival, is one way we measure progress, for example, through the United Nations Sustainable Development Goals.

A

United Nations Sustainable Development Goals are 17 targets for human development by 2030 – including access to clean water and decent work – which were set by member nations in 2015.

Thorsten Veblen was an American sociologist and economist. A critic of late-19th-century capitalism, he coined the phrase 'conspicuous consumption'.

Consumer capitalism is a term applied to an economic system reliant on generating consumer demand through marketing techniques that ground social status in buying rather than producing goods.

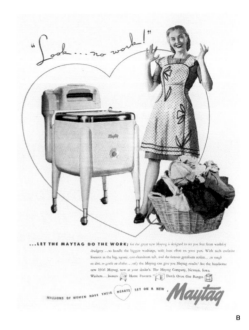

..."Look...no work!"

...LET THE MAYTAG DO THE WORK; for the great new Maytag is designed to set you free from washday drudgery...to handle the biggest washings, with least effort on your part. With such exclusive features as the big, square, cast-aluminum tub, and the famous gyrafoam action...so rough on dirt, so gentle on clothes...only the Maytag can give you Maytag results! See the handsome new 1946 Maytag, now at your dealer's. The Maytag Company, Newton, Iowa. Washers...Ironers 🔲 Home Freezers 🔲 Dutch Oven Gas Ranges 🔲

MILLIONS OF WOMEN HAVE THEIR HEARTS SET ON A NEW *Maytag*

B

In contrast, among the most privileged – those who American economist Thorsten Veblen (1857–1929) referred to as 'the Leisure Class' – success can be indicated not only by freedom from having to earn a wage, but by being able to have other people perform all the tasks you would rather avoid. Veblen was writing at the end of the American Gilded Age and drew parallels with the inequality and exploitation of monarchical systems. 'Groom of the stool' was a term applied during the Tudor period to members of the English royal court, whose sought-after duties are likely to have included wiping the monarch's bottom.

Reducing effortful work is also big business. Perhaps the greatest lifestyle benefit of consumer capitalism has been labour-saving devices ranging from electric kettles and vacuum cleaners to dishwashers. Indeed, reflecting on how domestic appliances can transform the workload of citizens, particularly women, the economist Ha-Joon Chang has argued that 'the washing machine is more important than the internet'. For better-off families in developed nations such devices were vital, as the habit of employing (female) domestic servants declined in the early twentieth century, and as more women entered the labour market from the 1960s onwards.

A The satisfactions
of consumerism are
fleeting but addictive.
The elation on receipt
of a new purchase or
a pay rise soon recedes
and the individual returns
to their normal set level
of happiness. The set
level of happiness does
not increase over time
with the accumulation
of more things or further
increases in pay.
B Training on exercise
bikes: professional and
white-collar employees
live largely sedentary
lives so have to under-
take physical activity
as an activity separate
from work.

Yet, even if there were no practical constraints on economic growth, it is difficult to imagine a world where most people could live without undertaking substantial labour. Devices may reduce the burden overall, but we must still empty the vacuum cleaner or clean the microwave. We might outsource our gardening or child-rearing, but we still need to find workers and give orders, as well as earning enough to pay them. As affluence rises and technology improves so do our expectations.

Social scientists Philip Brickman (1943–82) and Donald T. Campbell (1916–96) coined the term 'the hedonic treadmill' to describe how the satisfaction of meeting one set of needs is short lived, and lays the foundation for another set. The wider idea that 'the more we have, the more we want' was captured as long ago as 1754 by French philosopher Jean-Jacques Rousseau (1712–78). He wrote: 'Since these conveniences by becoming habitual had almost entirely ceased to be enjoyable, and at the same time degenerated into true needs, it became much more cruel to be deprived of them than to possess them was sweet, and men were unhappy to lose them without being happy to possess them.'

A

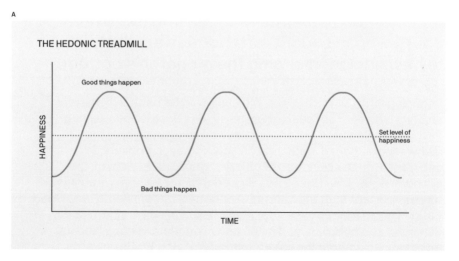

THE HEDONIC TREADMILL

Good things happen

HAPPINESS

Set level of happiness

Bad things happen

TIME

One of the ironies of modern life is how hard people work in paid employment to spend money on things that ostensibly make life easier. To achieve the level of physical fitness and appearance I expect as a middle-aged man involves a lot more work than my grandfather, who would not have dreamed of getting on an exercise bike or paying the dentist hundreds of pounds for a replacement crown. Also, an economy geared to continuous growth creates new burdens as we sort our rubbish into different recycling bins or schedule yoga or mindfulness sessions to dial down our stress levels.

Mindfulness applies to range of practices, generally forms of non-spiritual meditation, which train the mind to focus on the moment, thereby reducing anxiety and increasing wellbeing.

You may object that my fitness regime is not really 'work'; after all I do not get paid to do these things, nor am I forced to undertake them. They are my choice. But this reminds us of work as a reflection of intrinsic motivation. The Latin word '*opus*', used now mainly to designate a piece of classical music, means work in the sense of a 'work of art' or 'our life's work'. For some people work carries a sense of vocation, a calling based on their own abilities and needs and the change they want to bring about in the world. Implicit here is the idea that every life involves striving to be the best we can in whatever we choose to do, whether building a family business, creating art, living up to our political or religious principles or having a flat stomach at 60.

B

Each of these three ideas
of work – to earn, to live
and to thrive – brings with
them different perspectives
and issues.

Work as earning is central to debates
about the economy, social justice
and power. Materialist accounts
of history generally describe the main
stages of human development in terms
of systems of production and forms of
labour. Indeed, for each of the founding
figures of modern sociology, paid
work was pivotal to their world view.

A

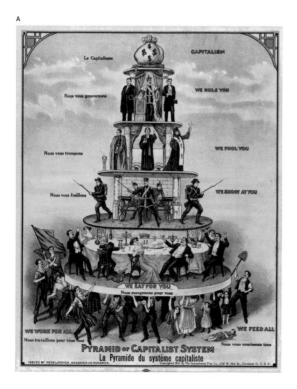

Materialism is a
philosophical and
historical perspective
that sees physical
matter as the basis
of reality and views
mental states as the
result of material
interactions.

**Protestant work
ethic** is the idea that
religious beliefs –
particularly those of
Calvinists – associate
activities such as work
and trade with moral
and spiritual value,
thus encouraging
capitalist enterprise.

A   This 1911 satirical cartoon entitled 'Pyramid of Capitalist System', and attributed to Nedljkovich, Brashich and Kuharich, depicts a social hierarchy pyramid with the wealthy few at the top enjoying the fruits of the labours of the many workers at the bottom who 'work for all'. Karl Marx was among the economists who saw labour as the basis of all economic value.

B   Soviet poster 'He who doesn't work, doesn't eat', issued in Uzbekistan in 1920. Both communist and capitalist systems have extolled the virtues of hard work.

B

Building on the ideas of British economists David Ricardo (1772–1823) and Adam Smith (1723–90), Karl Marx (1818–83) saw labour as the ultimate source of economic value and the basis of class relations and exploitation. Emile Durkheim (1858–1917) singled out the division of labour as the key to understanding the nature of modern society. Max Weber (1864–1920) identified the Protestant work ethic as the motor of capitalist development. Today, when we describe the health or progress of a national or local economy, levels of employment, remuneration and vocational skills are among the primary measures.

The idea of work as the burdens involved in day-to-day life features in discussions on technology or lifestyle. Advertisers promise their goods or services will make life easier, saving time, reducing drudgery and complication. Today's citizens of affluent countries are less likely to find themselves required to do back-breaking physical work to sustain themselves but will often complain about the complexity of modern living. Digital technology has reduced the amount of effort involved in many activities, ranging from finding out information to renewing your driving licence, but it has also arguably generated new work as we take responsibility for tasks which might previously have been performed by bank workers or travel agents. As many people came to recognize during COVID-19 lockdown, commuting to and from work – for which we are not paid – can be one of the most onerous burdens of modern life. More profoundly, many people in middle age now find themselves caring both for children unable to be economical independent and their ageing parents.

A   Front cover of
*The Complete Book
of Self-Sufficiency*
by John Seymour,
published in 1976
during the height of
the self-sufficiency
movement in the UK.

B   Decorative plates
commemorating the
British miners strike
of 1984–85. For many,
this was the last,
forlorn stand against
de-industrialization.

The demands of modern living have led people to try to escape the pressures and expectations of a modern economy. The self-sufficiency movement grew in the 1970s, and some of those with the means to down-size, become 'out of towners' or go 'off the grid' to reduce complexity and the insistent pace of modern life.

Work as thriving or the path to fulfilment carries moral weight. The reasons for work may be primarily extrinsic, such as compulsion or remuneration, but often other motivations are involved. Religious perspectives on work tend to eschew instrumentalism and focus on ideas of self-discipline and duty to community or God. It is an idea often associated with the Protestant work ethic, a driving force in the emergence of capitalism. In Catholic Social Teaching, the duty of employers and governments to uphold the dignity of workers is balanced with the injunction that workers must 'fully and fairly' perform their duties.

A

Catholic Social Teaching is a set of principles concerning the common good and human dignity, including in work. Its origins lie in the encyclical letter *Rerum Novarum* issued by Pope Leo XIII in 1891.

Post-materialism is a phrase coined by political scientist Ronald Inglehart in 1977 and refers to a set of values prizing self-expression and life quality over material acquisition and consumerism.

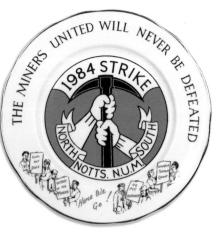

The fact that someone will pay us to do something shows that what we are doing is at some level valued by our fellow citizens. The non-monetary rewards of a job like teaching may be obvious, but during the COVID-19 crisis the global behemoth Amazon – often associated with intensive and low-paid work – ran adverts narrated by warehouse workers in which they emphasized the satisfaction of making sure people receive their on-line orders. As an example of what Ronald Inglehart and the World Values Survey has identified as a post-materialist turn in the values of liberal democracies, it is frequently argued that millennials and younger generations are more concerned with meaning and purpose at work.

In recent years social scientists and politicians have been reminded of the importance to people of a sense of agency and shared identity. Work can be an important source of both. Arguably, the terrible impact on so many working class communities of the decline in manufacturing in the UK and other industrialized countries in the 1980s was not only about the loss of a steady income, it also meant that workers – mainly men – lost the sense of solidarity and collective pride associated with employment in sectors like mining, steel making and engineering.

A

Medieval **guilds** were associations of craft workers or tradespeople who regulated work in their field within a particular geographical area.

In **video games** getting the level of difficulty right is a key design feature. 'Dynamic game difficulty balancing' uses machine learning to adapt the challenge of a game to the player in real time.

A In *A Goldsmith in his Shop*, 1449, Petrus Christus portrays the goldsmith's virtuosity and precision. The idea of craft carries positive connotations of status, skill and satisfaction.

B 'Flow' – a happy and focused state – results from a task having the right balance of challenge and ability, allowing high engagement.

A more intrinsic view of fulfilling work focuses on the skills involved. There is the idea of 'craft' which became an important organizing principle in the middle ages with the rise of guilds, and in the modern world with the idea of professionalism. For many occupational groups, for example teaching and nursing, achieving professional status has been a route to higher pride, social status and remuneration.

Someone might enjoy the standing and bargaining power of being a doctor or accountant but still find the work itself stressful or boring. A different, arguably higher, work aspiration is enjoyment of the activity itself.

In 1991 the Hungarian American psychologist Mihaly Csikszentmihalyi introduced the concept of 'flow', a state of wellbeing resulting from complete immersion in an activity. Many activities can induce flow, but according to Csikszentmihalyi it tends to involve autonomy, clarity of purpose and clear feedback. Flow is not effortless. Instead it comes from the right balance of achievement and challenge.

The insight that our enjoyment of an activity involves the appropriate level of effort has helped to shape the design of various teaching methods and products, including video games in which each new level is a little, but not too much, harder than the one preceding it. But the activities most often cited as enabling a sense of flow, such as playing a musical instrument, gardening and craft work suggest there may be a physical component. If our capacity to lose ourselves in effortful activity is a prehistorically evolved response it would have developed at a time when most work involved engaging directly with nature. American philosopher Matthew Crawford, who combines his academic role with running a motorbike repair shop, has argued that working with resistant material objects provides a form of satisfaction and release from self-obsession that is unavailable from work which only involves abstract thought, interpersonal communication or the manipulation of digital information.

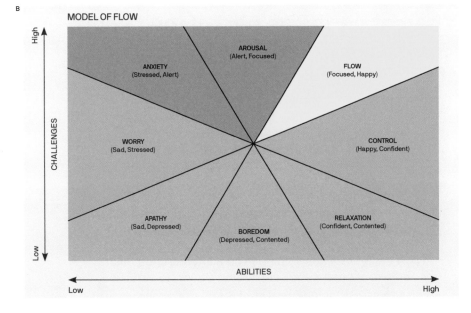

B

MODEL OF FLOW

High

CHALLENGES

Low

ANXIETY
(Stressed, Alert)

AROUSAL
(Alert, Focused)

FLOW
(Focused, Happy)

WORRY
(Sad, Stressed)

CONTROL
(Happy, Confident)

APATHY
(Sad, Depressed)

BOREDOM
(Depressed, Contented)

RELAXATION
(Confident, Contented)

ABILITIES

Low   High

A Mid-19th-century photographs of slave wet nurses with their owners' infants. Wet-nursing has been common practice among aristocrats through the ages and among slave owners, including those of the American South.

B Care work is becoming ever more vital to the economy and an ageing society but it continues to suffer low pay and status.

Ada Peters Brown aged 7 months – left 3 days

A

Across history the boundaries between different conceptions and categories of work have shifted and blurred in significant ways. The obvious example is care which exists simultaneously as work we want to do, work we have to do and work we get paid to do. A carer could be a low-paid employee, a parent caring as part of their social role, or a volunteer seeking a sense of self-worth and fulfilment.

From what we can tell, the care of children and elders was a collective responsibility in the solidaristic prehistoric world of the hunter gatherer, although it is likely that the group's mothers and grandmothers did the lion's share. As people moved into a more sedentary life on the land or in fixed settlements, care generally became the responsibility of the extended family. Nevertheless, throughout history the burdensome and low-status aspects of looking after people has been underlined by society's elites who have consistently used the efforts of other people, including slaves, to perform duties ranging from teaching to wet-nursing.

A **volunteer's** labour to individuals and organizations is hard to define or measure precisely but a 2018 UN study estimated its global scale to be equivalent to 109 million full-time workers.

Commodification refers to the process whereby an activity, previously outside the formal economy, is turned into a tradable resource.

Today a combination of family choices, economic trends and social policy has brought about the **commodification** of care. Indeed, if we include the education of children, something most people undertook as a familial and subsistence obligation in the past, care is now by far the largest occupational activity in the labour market of industrialized countries. The scale of care and the scope for it to grow both through the needs of an ageing population and the desires of an affluent one, is one reason to be sceptical about the idea that we are approaching a workless future.

B

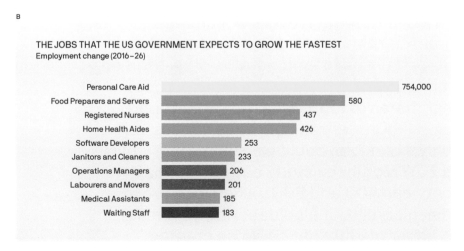

THE JOBS THAT THE US GOVERNMENT EXPECTS TO GROW THE FASTEST
Employment change (2016–26)

Personal Care Aid	754,000
Food Preparers and Servers	580
Registered Nurses	437
Home Health Aides	426
Software Developers	253
Janitors and Cleaners	233
Operations Managers	206
Labourers and Movers	201
Medical Assistants	185
Waiting Staff	183

Before the global shock of the COVID-19 pandemic there was a great deal of speculation among experts, business leaders and governments about the future of paid work. Many commentators assume the future will be a function primarily of technological change. Digital technology and the growth and speed of data processing has already had major effects on the labour market: reducing the need for routine clerical work and changing the nature of skilled work in sectors ranging from design to banking. The onset of machine learning (what people tend to mean by Artificial Intelligence/AI) is predicted to have much more far reaching consequences. Similarly, intelligent robotics has the potential to accelerate processes of automation that have radically reduced manufacturing employment in industrialized countries.

One of the first detailed analyses of the likely impact of these technologies on future work, and one which shaped much of the subsequent debate, was published in 2013 by Oxford-based academics Carl B. Frey and Michael A. Osborne. Their research into the components of a range of different occupations came up with the headline grabbing conclusion that nearly half (47%) of jobs in the United States were at high risk of automation over the coming 20 years. Since Frey and Osborne's analysis there have been innumerable other studies, most of which have made more modest estimates of job losses. An OECD report of 21 industrialized countries suggested only 9% of jobs could be automated, while a 2017 McKinsey study suggested that between 400 and 800 million jobs are at risk globally but also described a similar number of jobs that could be created.

As in previous periods of technological change, a focus on job loss has led to both pessimistic and utopian visions of the future of work. The former predict a world of mass unemployment, economic hardship and social conflict; the latter, including 'post-workist' thinkers like Canadian philosopher Nick Srnicek envisage a society liberated from employment and the compulsion and power relations that come with it. Some radical left commentators have summoned the ideal of 'fully automated luxury communism'.

In this they echo Karl Marx's vision of a post-capitalist world where work is varied and freely chosen: 'to hunt in the morning, fish in the afternoon, rear cattle in the evening, criticize after dinner, just as I have a mind, without ever becoming hunter, fisherman, herdsman or critic' (from *The German Ideology*).

A Programmable industrial robots, such as those seen here working on an electric vehicle assembly line, have already reduced employment in the heavy manufacturing sector and are now displacing workers in other areas. Unlike workers, robots do not pay tax.

B Some jobs are highly vulnerable to automation. This Amazon fufilment centre in Florida, USA, which opened in 2018, uses hundreds of robots to pick and pack items. The robots can lift as much as 340kg (750 lb) and can drive 1.5m (5 ft) per second.

A

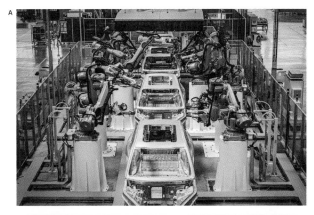

B

A

B

John Maynard Keynes

was the most important
economist of the 20th
century and his ideas
continue to be highly
influential today. He
was also a classicist,
historian and patron
of the arts.

National insurance,

or social insurance,
systems exist in most
developed countries
and involve workers
making contributions to
funds managed by the
state or other agencies
which bring a range of
welfare entitlements.

A   Unemployed US workers wearing
sandwich boards advertising
their willingness to work on
the streets of Chicago in 1934.

B   The Great Depression of
the 1930s, and the mass
unemployment that resulted,
devastated communities and
families. Many fear modern
technology could lead to
a similar outcome today.

C   This graph shows the rapid and
largely unexpected decline in
UK unemployment following the
global financial crisis of 2008.

Such futurism is not restricted to
revolutionaries. Perhaps reflecting his
own broad intellectual interests, the
great liberal economist John Maynard
Keynes (1883–1946) delivered a lecture
during the economic turmoil of 1930
entitled 'Economic possibilities for our
grandchildren'. If Keynes had grandchildren,
they would now be in their seventies or
eighties and able to compare today's
economy to his prediction of a world of
leisure: 'Thus for the first time since his
creation man will be faced with his real,
his permanent problem – how to use his
freedom from pressing economic cares,
how to occupy the leisure, which science
and compound interest will have won for
him, to live wisely and agreeably and well.'

**Keynes may have been awry
in his predictions, but he
recognized that while technological advances enable
new possibilities, including
choosing leisure, the nature
of work also depends on
political, economic and
social choices.**

It is an irony of the many recent technology-based predictions about a jobless future that they were published during an era of recovery following the global financial economic crisis of 2008 during which, in many industrialized economies, unemployment was falling and the proportion of the adult population in work rising. Indeed, in 2019 the UK employment rate reached 76.2%, the highest ever recorded.

Even if technology could make many jobs redundant there are surely other reasons societies need most adults to undertake paid work? The most obvious are economic. In developed countries taxes on employment and earnings are a large part of the revenues necessary to fund state activities, ranging from national defence to education and health care. In the UK, for example, in 2019 the combination of income tax and national insurance (levied on employers and employees) raised around 45% of government revenue. Also, the process through which labour is combined with other factors of production to generate value is the source of business income and profit and therefore, surely, essential to the functioning of capitalism.

c

PERCENTAGE OF UK POPULATION AGED 16–64 IN WORK
(1971–2019)

75.8%

PERCENTAGE IN WORK

80

75

70

65

60

1970   1980   1990   2000   2010   2019

YEAR

But are these economic factors immutable? After all, tax revenues differ greatly from country to country and historically. In Europe, the highest marginal income tax rate varies from 10% in Bosnia and 15% in Hungary to over 55% in Denmark and Finland. Today in the US, income and social insurance tax account for well over half of Federal income but in the early twentieth century the Federal government did not raise revenue from employment relying instead entirely on taxes on goods (largely on imports) and property. There are also new ways to generate revenue. Environmental taxes achieve the double benefit of generating revenue and incentivizing sustainable business practices. They have been growing slowly but steadily and now make up over 6% of government revenues across the EU. If we are serious about responding to the climate emergency this figure will need to get a lot higher. Reflecting the changing nature of our economy, there have been many proposals to tax data. Microsoft founder Bill Gates is amongst those who have called for a tax on robots.

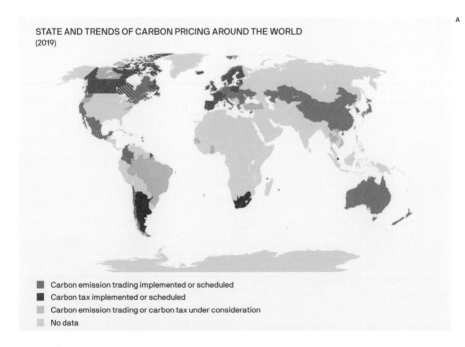

STATE AND TRENDS OF CARBON PRICING AROUND THE WORLD (2019)

- ■ Carbon emission trading implemented or scheduled
- ■ Carbon tax implemented or scheduled
- Carbon emission trading or carbon tax under consideration
- No data

Environmental taxes seek to raise revenue while also disincentivizing activities that damage the local or global environment; examples range from carbon taxes to charges for the use of plastic bags.

A   Environmental taxes on carbon emissions or other forms of consumption, pollution and waste are likely to grow over the coming decades.

B   A German car worker assembling an electric SUV at the Volkswagen factory in Zwickau. It is one of two electric models the company hopes will take a high market share.

C   A steel worker in a Brandenburg steel plant. In future taxes may focus less on employment and more on carbon emissions, such as those from steel plants.

It would be challenging and take time, but there is no reason why states could not come to rely much less on work as a source of income.

As for the functioning of a market economy, it is worth noting that capitalism has thrived with very different levels of work activity. Before COVID-19 the main measure of employment levels – the Labour Force Participation Rate – ranged from 80% in the UK to 61% in the US to 51% in Greece. In working an average 1,400 hours a year, the highly productive German workforce put in only three quarters as much time as the average American. Overall, working hours in developed nations today are between a third and half of the levels of the nineteenth century. Indeed, although still working longer than prehistoric people, we are now much closer to historical estimates of the average working hours of the period before the Industrial Revolution.

A

A The Googleplex HQ and Facebook offices in California. To attract and retain the best talent IT giants such as Google and Facebook offer high wages and worker-friendly conditions.

B Paying to be fed: an aerial view of cars queuing for a McDonald's drive-through in Swansea. UK consumer spending on catering doubled between 1997 and 2019, one reason why the COVID lockdowns hit the economy so hard.

At the firm level, tech businesses – most notably Google and Facebook – generate massive profits and market share with relatively small workforces. In 2019 the average Google employee in the UK earned £226,000 and presumably generated a great deal more than this in revenue. There is no reason why a capitalist economy could not make profits from a smaller, high-value labour force working fewer aggregate and individual hours than is the norm today.

Neither the need for government revenue nor for corporate profits are insurmountable barriers to radical change in the nature of work. A more fundamental factor lies in the division of labour. Emile Durkheim saw this as the critical shift to modernity.

Indeed, for Durkheim the interdependence that develops with the division of labour is a source of solidarity in modern societies. Peasant households might grow from seed the food they ate and sold, manage nearly all their own subsistence needs including building and maintaining their homes and educate and provide care to their family members, but modern citizens rely on a vast array of products and services which it would be impossible to provide for ourselves.

The growing **division of labour** into more specialized employment tasks is a characteristic of modern societies and the basis for trade and domestic and global economic interdependence.

A **subsistence** economy refers to one in which most economic activity is directed to meeting basis human needs (food, shelter, clothing) rather than generating goods for market. Such economies are assumed to be very poor.

If you consider an average day involving putting on your shop-bought clothes, using soap and shampoo in the shower, eating, travelling, using public services, accessing the internet and its services, checking out your bank balance, having a meal in a restaurant and watching a box set in bed. All of this relies on a complex division of labour involving large groups of specialist functions and services. Even those who chose a very simple life would be unable to operate, be full citizens or even obey the law, without depending on the work of others.

The **American New Deal** of the 1930s was a series of public work projects, reforms, and regulations introduced by President Franklin D. Roosevelt in response to the Great Depression of the United States.

Disposable income is the money an individual or family has left to spend when they have paid taxes, social security, rent or the mortage, the food bill and other essential outgoings.

Labour markets change. In the post-war period a large proportion of the population was involved in primary industry and manufacturing; who would then have predicted full employment when those sectors had dwindled to a small fraction of the workforce? There are many parts of society where extra jobs would be useful and welcome. The UK government, for example, could employ another million plus people immediately to improve health and social care, widen educational and cultural opportunities, rebuild infra-structure and enhance public spaces.

A

A Two posters printed by the Works Progress Adminstration in the USA between 1936 and 1941, encouraging labourers to work for America and to gain confidence from their work. The American New Deal helped end the depression and provided new jobs in areas ranging from farming to the arts.

B Activists from the Sunrise Movement and Justice Democrats leave the House Minority Leader Nancy Pelosi's office to be arrested on Capitol Hill in Washington, DC, in November 2018. The protesters were demanding that Pelosi, if elected Speaker of the House, create a new select committee on climate change.

C Representatives Alexandra Ocasio-Cortez and Ed Markey support campaigners calling for a Green New Deal in Washington, DC, February 2019. Some of these measures are being enacted by President Biden.

Indeed, this is largely how the American New Deal addressed the mass unemployment of the thirties. Moreover, if every person had the disposable income they could make the same choices as other well-off people: employ a cleaner, a personal trainer, have a weekly massage or beauty treatment, maybe even take on a yoga instructor, life coach or therapist (jobs which have little immediate prospect of being automated). We cannot all be celebrities or sports stars, but they often employ a whole entourage of coaches, advisors and assistants. With enough disposable income our desire for other people's labour seems inexhaustible.

Work will change again in the future just as it has in the past....

A

The **Neolithic Revolution,** also known as the Agricultural Revolution, began about 12,000 years ago and marked the shift from hunting and gathering to the domestication of animals and the development of agriculture.

Thomas Hobbes was a Western philosopher. He is most well known for his book *Leviathan* (1651), which laid the foundations for contract theory.

From Stone Age hunter-gatherers to modern gig workers the nature of human work has been transformed over time. While this chapter is inevitably broad brush, and largely eurocentric, it reminds us that the way we think about work in modern industrialized societies is distinctive and, in historical terms, recent. While technological change has been a significant force, the nature of work also reflects and reinforces the belief systems and distribution of power in society. If we want better work for all, it will be part of creating a better society.

There are two limited but fascinating sources of information on the nature of prehistoric work; one growing the other declining. First, the expanding archaeological record of life before the Neolithic Revolution, which saw the emergence of the first mass civilizations in the fertile crescent of Eurasia around ten to twelve thousand years ago. Second, what we have learned and can learn from the lives of the dwindling band of traditional societies in remote regions that have avoided, or been bypassed, by modernity.

B

An **anthropologist** is a scientist of humanity. Anthropologists examine archaeology, language, biology and culture to study what makes us human, and how we have evolved.

A Bushmen have lived in the Kalahari Desert for millennia. Today there are approximately 100,000 Bushmen across southern Africa, mainly in South Africa, Botswana, Namibia and Zambia.

B Game playing among the San tribe in the Kalahari Desert. Evidence from groups like this suggest that members of prehistoric societies worked fewer hours than modern people.

For many centuries after the Enlightenment the predominant view of prehistoric life was summed up in the famous phrase of English philosopher Thomas Hobbes (1588 – 1679): 'nasty, brutish and short'. This assumption has come under sustained critique. Not only does it now seem that violence was quite rare among prehistoric groups, but also that our hunter-gatherer ancestors may have had a better work-life balance than us. Researchers studying the Kalahari bushmen found that adults spent no more than two or three days a week hunting. The influential anthropologist Marshall Sahlins based his assertion that our distant ancestors were the 'original affluent society' on observing the African Hadza people who limited their hunting to two hours a day and spent most of their time in various forms of play.

What the study of prehistory can tell us about attitudes or cultures is limited. However, discoveries have challenged the view of Stone Age humans, or even their Neanderthal cousins, as rudimentary scavengers. Our ancestors may have started using tools millions of years ago. The horse butchery site discovered in Boxgrove in the south of England, and estimated to be 500,000 years old, included tools made by the species *Homo heidelbergensis*, a possible ancestor for modern humans and Neanderthals. Making the flint hand axes found at the site would have involved considerable skill. Paintings in the Chauvet Cave in the Ardèche, France, show artistic skill and endeavour that dates back at least 30,000 years. The prehistoric record now includes evidence of house-building, religious rituals, textile weaving and some trading.

It is becoming clear that prehistoric work was skilled and varied. There would have been an allocation of tasks and a division of labour, including presumably some age and gender differentiation based, for example, on physical strength and women nursing infants. But, in contrast to what was to come, there is little to suggest that one group of people was expected to work for another. Effort was undertaken for the survival of the community not the advancement of the individual. Among the key factors constraining the emergence of work as a power relation would have been the relatively small size of groups and a nomadic subsistence lifestyle which gave few opportunities for the accumulation of any form of wealth.

A   Flints discovered on a site near Boxgrove in Sussex, England, which appears to have been chosen as a place to corral, butcher and feast on the meat of wild horses.

B   Figurative cave paintings in the Ardèche department of southern France are amongst the best preserved in the world. Featuring at least 13 different species of animals, partial human figures, scenes and suggestions of movement, the paintings are exceptional for their time.

A

Accumulation is the process of increasing assets or wealth over time, beyond those needed for immediate consumption. In ancient times, this might have meant hoarding precious goods.

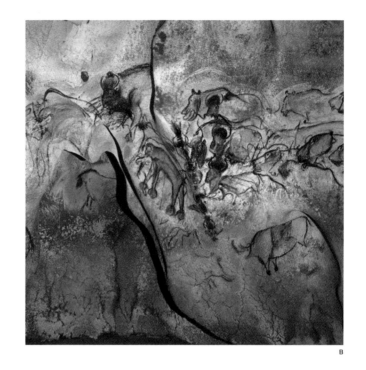

B

The vast majority of human time on earth has been characterized by the hunter-gatherer lifestyle, but things change dramatically when people settle on the land. Settlements and groups become larger, agricultural productivity increases and the first mass civilizations emerge. By making a surplus possible, advances in agriculture create the conditions for inequality as certain individuals and groups accumulate wealth. The privileged no longer have to do their share of the work.

A

Debt bondage is work exchanged for a debt that can ultimately never be paid. Threats, violence, imprisonment and other brutal tactics are often used to ensure the victim cannot leave or seek help.

Edward Colston was an English merchant. His local philanthropic activities were marked in various Bristol place names and monuments but his connections with the Atlantic slave trade have led to a critical reappraisal of his life.

The scene is set for the emergence of the first and most brutal form of labour relation. Surpluses create the incentives for oppression, but slavery also relies on systematic differences in power between different groups and on religious, racial or martial ideologies that legitimize exploitation. The common theme in all forms of slavery is the perception of some human beings as mere commodities to be owned, used in just about any way their owners want (including sexual exploitation) and sold. Indeed, in part to justify the behaviour of their owners, enslaved people are generally not seen as full human beings.

A Tunisian mosaics from the 3rd and 4th century, showing slaves serving at a banquet in Dougga and helping their mistress with her toilette in Sidi Ghrib. Today 40 million people are estimated to be enslaved worldwide, 1 in 4 of them children, and almost three-quarters women and girls.

B Black Lives Matter protesters topple the statue of slave owner Edward Colston, pushing it into the River Avon on 7 June 2020 in Bristol, England. The city's wealth was built on the slave trade and Colston was one of its main benefactors.

People become enslaved through being captured in war and conquest, through debt bondage, punishment for crime or simply being born enslaved. There is evidence of slavery in almost all ancient civilizations; from Rome to China, from Greece to the ancient Americas. In many societies, enslaved people have made up a large proportion, sometimes even a majority, of the population. It is estimated that most households in ancient Greece owned at least one enslaved person. The slave trade has been a major motor of geopolitics, trade and economic development throughout history. Countless millions of people have lost their liberty, or never known freedom, and have endured appalling conditions and injustices.

We tend to think of slavery as something in the distant past but, in some places, it was only abolished in the twentieth century, remaining legal in Mauritania until 2007. It is estimated that today around 40 million people, many of them children, are enslaved around the world. Even in the UK, whose former prime minister Theresa May took a lead internationally on tackling modern slavery, it is estimated that around 100,000 people are victims. The anti-racist demand to remove statues commemorating the lives of those who became rich through slavery – for example Edward Colston (1636–1721) in Bristol – has drawn attention to how the slave trade and the racist ideology that legitimated it continues to cast a shadow over modern societies.

B

The **transatlantic slave trade** involved Europeans transporting enslaved African people to the Americas. There they were forced to produce goods, such as sugar or tobacco, that were returned to Europe.

The conditions of slavery have varied. The Roman empire was built on slavery and – some argue – was ultimately enfeebled by its reliance on it. But some Roman slaves were employed in skilled crafts and professions, and could even own property. The relative comfort of this class of enslaved people contrasts with the abject plight of the twelve million African people transported to the Caribbean and Americas through the transatlantic slave trade, of whom an estimated two million died in transit.

An appreciation of the scale and importance of slavery can fit into two contrasting narratives about history and work. One is a story of progress from slavery in the ancient world to feudalism in the medieval world to gradually more humane forms of employment from industrialization up to today. From this further stages in a progressive journey of human dignity and opportunity might confidently be predicted.

A

Marchand d'Esclaves de Gorée

B

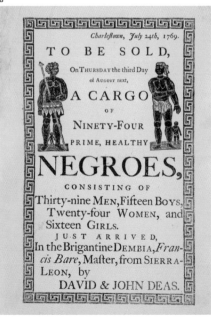

A *Slave traders in Gorés* by Jacques Grasset de Saint-Sauveur: the island of Gorée off the coast of Senegal was the largest slave-trading centre on the African coast from the 15th to the 19th century.

B Handbill advertising a slave auction in Charleston, South Carolina, in 1769. One in six slaves transported in the transatlantic slave trade died in transit.

C Medieval illustration of peasants harvesting wheat in August. In Europe between the 9th and 15th centuries peasants were feudal workers, bound to the land and owned by the feudal lord or king.

An alternative interpretation – favoured, for example, by Marxist thinkers – would emphasize the continuities between legal slavery and 'wage slavery' as the expression of different forms of exploitative class relations. The employment contract requires today's employees to do what they are told, while the distribution of resources in society means that most people must work in order to be able to subsist and participate. From this perspective, only the abolition of the power dynamic of labour relations as part of a wider social transformation can free work from its associations with oppression.

Paid employment has been the dominant form of labour relation in the developed world for less than two centuries; feudalism – the predominant model of the Middle Ages – lasted at least four times as long. Typically, feudal workers received little or no pay but were allowed to farm their masters' land or keep a proportion of their own produce in exchange for their labour.

The **Japanese shogun system** was both hierarchical and hereditary, and prevailed under the rule of emperors from the 12th to the 19th century.

The **Black Death** killed up to 60% of Europe's entire population between 1346 and 1353. It was an epidemic of bubonic plague, a disease caused by bacteria carried by rats and rat fleas. The plague's spread was exacerbated by merchant ships travelling between Asia and Europe. The plague caused religious, economic and social upheaval.

One of the best known **caste systems** is in India, in which people are grouped into four classes: *Brahmins*, priests; *Kshatriyas*, rulers; *Vaishyas*, merchants or farmers; and *Shudras*, labourers, and others outside the system regarded as untouchables. It arose as the Mughal Empire collapsed (1850s), and was exacerbated by British colonial rule, in which rigid segregation underpinned appointments to senior roles.

Western accounts of feudalism tend to focus on its form in countries like Britain, but similar characteristics can be seen in other global regions, including the Japanese shogun system and in various colonial practices. The more authoritarian form of serf feudalism that spread to eastern Europe in the late Middle Ages persisted well into the nineteenth century.

Labour relations under feudalism reflected a social system which was politically decentralized, socially hierarchical, religiously conformist and, in comparison to the post-industrial era, economically cyclical rather than expansionary. The origins of feudalism lay in the need of rulers – whose territories comprised a set of private kingdoms more than a modern state – for protection from various external threats. In the western European model, through a typically four-tiered system of king, baron, knight and peasant, land was exchanged for loyalty, military service, taxes, services and good. The stratified reciprocity of the feudal relationship and the emphasis on service distinguishes it from tributary systems more common in other regions in which peasants owned the land independently but were required to pay produce or taxes to higher authorities including the state or conquering powers.

The experiences of common people varied across the feudal period. For example, the bargaining power of peasants and itinerant farm labourers was significantly enhanced by labour shortages following the Black Death in the mid-fourteenth century. This shift in power has also been linked to the Peasant's Revolt of 1381, one of several such rebellions during the feudal era. Nevertheless, despite the profound inequality and denial of freedom inherent in feudalism it was a system legitimized by an account of the good of society.

A   Painting of a samurai on horseback, wearing armour. Shoguns, a form of military government, led Japan until the 19th century. The system had some feudal elements.

B   A 14th-century depiction of a knight by Pacino di Buonaguida. The feudal system was based on a strict hierarchy of roles and status.

As long as they met the obligations they had towards their vassal, peasants generally had rights to land, including common pasture or woodland, and some freedom over how they used their time and produce. Also, unlike most forms of slavery, there is an element of reciprocity in feudal labour relations. Upheld by a powerful Church, the medieval world view sees society as an integrated, hierarchical system in which each part should perform the role ordained for it. In contrast to the disdain for paid or onerous work among ancient elites, the Christian ideology of feudalism, like religiously sanctioned caste systems in other global regions and eras, extolled the dignity of labour at the same time as upholding the power relations which kept peasants in their place.

A

B

A

Aristotle was an ancient Greek polymath. He is generally considered the father of Western philosophy.

St Thomas Aquinas was an Italian Dominican monk and philosopher. A highly influential figure in theology, his ideas formed the basis for the Thomist school of thought.

Goldman Sachs is one of the largest investment banks in the world. It received (and repaid) a $10 billion investment from the US Treasury following its involvement in the sub-prime mortgage crisis of 2007–08. It was criticized for paying 953 employees bonuses of at least $1m each during the same period.

The peasant class, in which the whole family would work together both in the fields and maintaining subsistence, made up the vast majority of the workforce in largely agrarian economies like Britain. But in the Middle Ages, and throughout history, there have been other significant occupational groups. Among these are merchants, craft workers, members of religious communities, soldiers and those working at the margins of society.

Whilst medieval economies were largely local in character with rural areas producing goods for local towns and buying products from local tradespeople, merchants earned an income from moving goods between towns, regions and, sometimes, continents while providing or using rudimentary financial services. Merchants could become wealthy and their interests and the goods and revenues generated by trade would come to be influential in shaping the agendas of local and national rulers.

However, the attitude of the medieval church to commerce was ambivalent. Not only were there prohibitions against money-lending and the charging of interest (usury) but the very idea of financial profit making was frowned upon. The economy was not seen as an independent system with its own logic and imperatives but as part of a moral universe and subject to the same codes. Although the judgemental rhetoric of religious leaders often contrasted with the extensive financial dealings of the Church hierarchy, theological disapproval finds an echo in modern perceptions of finance as being parasitical on the 'real economy'. The ethical view of Aristotle (385–22 BC) and St Thomas Aquinas (1225–74) that it is suspect to make money from money began to lose its power in the late medieval period, but it has a twenty-first century version in journalist Matt Taibbi's vivid description in 2009 of Goldman Sachs as a 'vampire squid'.

A second significant group comprises artisans, craft workers and skilled tradesmen. They would generally run family businesses, owning their own property with workers including apprentices becoming part of the household. The forming of guilds covering a wide variety of activities provided workers with mutual protection and some control over competition, prices and standards.

A   Miniature from *Livre du régime des princes* by Gilles de Rome (1247–1316), showing Philippe the Bel (above) and adjacent scenes of a group of merchants and peasants working in the fields (below).
B   Sculptures of Saint Eligius, the patron saint of goldsmiths and other metal workers (left), and the Four Crowned Martyrs (right) by Nanni di Banco (1384–1421). Both sculptures were commissioned by the guilds of Florence for external niches of Orsanmichele, Florence, Italy. Guilds protected the economic interests and social status of crafts.

B

While many of these trades declined after industrialization, the philosophy and methods of guilds can be seen as the precursor to the principles underlying today's professional groups. Guild members might grow reasonably wealthy and even aspire to join the aristocracy. There would also have been a class of itinerant labourers – including traveller groups – able to pick up work in times of high demand but often suffering acute insecurity and poverty at a time when charity dispensed by the church was the only welfare system. Waged employment existed, as it did in the ancient world, but, apart from major European manufacturing centres like Flanders and Florence, it was generally in very small enterprises.

The church was the major employer and landholder in the medieval era with monastic life being attractive not only for reasons of faith but because it offered relative safety and economic security. Throughout history there have also been martial societies where the primary means of achieving the necessities of life has been through war and conquest.

A

B

A   Interior of J. Plater's Cart, Van and Carriage Works, Haddenham, Buckinghamshire, 1903. The craftsmen are grouped together in the workshop with their equipment. Two of the apprentices are young boys.

B   A group of Benedictine monks in County Limerick, Ireland, head off to work in the fields, 1936. Monks live an enclosed life, with routines involving silence, prayer and physical work. Individual monks are poor, but monasteries can be wealthy institutions.

C   This painting by Georg Emanuel Opitz (1775–1841) entitled *Le no 113 Palais-Royal*, 1815, depicts prostitutes in Paris plying their trade with military officers.

Gender power relations refers to the set of roles, attitudes and behaviours that society decides is appropriate to men and women. This can be either the cause or consequence of unequal power relations.

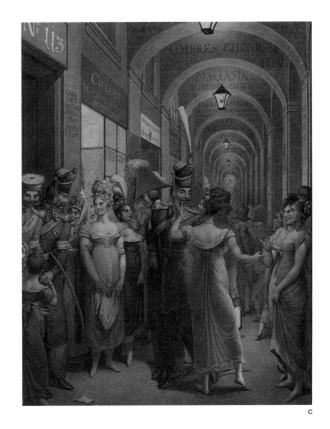

c

A proportion of those under arms have been paid mercenaries. Nevertheless, the ideas of pride, loyalty to lord, land or faith associate military and religious work with purpose or vocation beyond material instrumentality, ideals which continue to be associated with fulfilment in work.

A further category of workers includes those whose tasks have been associated with disgust or taboo – for example dealing with human waste or corpses – leading those who undertake them to be pushed to the margins of society. The most significant and ubiquitous example is prostitution, sometimes described as 'the world's oldest profession'. Whilst not all sex workers have been women, the prevalence of prostitution from the ancient world to today (research in 2012 estimated 42 million work in the sex trade globally) and its status, including the widespread persecution of prostitutes, is a reminder of the importance of gender power relations in the history of work. In many countries debate rages between those who want to extend the protections available to other employees to prostitutes and those who believe it to be so inherently dangerous and degrading that sex work, including those who manage it and procure it, should continue to be criminalized.

A

The late Middle Ages saw the rise of the mercantile practices and commercial and cultural attitudes which laid the foundations for the subsequent emergence of industrialization. The subsequent development of work is a complex process happening in different ways and at different times in each country. But key aspects of the 250-year journey, from the first Industrial Revolution to today, shed light on current choices.

One is the impact of technological disruption, mediated, as always, by power relations and ideology.

In Britain and many other countries, the most acute example occurred as industrialization gathered pace. This was a period which saw the decline of feudal arrangements and the enclosures of common or peasant land within larger commercial farming estates, along with the proletarianizing of many skilled craft workers and small traders. This process culminated in Britain in the desperate living conditions experienced by factory worker households in mid-nineteenth century industrial towns and cities.

The word Luddite is now generally used disparagingly to describe someone vainly standing in the way of technological advances. But the Luddite rebellion took place in the midst of the period of early British industrialization between 1790 and 1840, described by historian Robert C. Allen as 'Engel's pause'; when working-class wages stagnated and living conditions declined even while national GDP (Gross Domestic Product) rose substantially. The phrase is named after Karl Marx's collaborator on the *Communist Manifesto*, Frederich Engels (1820–95), author of *The Conditions of the Working Class in England* (1845), which was one of number of exposés of the life faced by the impoverished inhabitants of early industrial cities.

Mercantile means trading, or buying and selling, products to earn money. The first known use of the word was in 1638.

Proletarianizing is downward social mobility; notably used by Karl Marx to describe the process of artisans and other sections of the middle class becoming working class.

Luddites, radical English textile workers, destroyed machinery in protests against manufacturers who used machines to undermine labour practices between 1811 and 1816. They feared technology would make their skills redundant.

GDP (Gross Domestic Product) is the main measure of the size and growth of activity in the formal economy.

B

C

Some commentators have drawn parallels between this period and the stagnation of wages for those in the bottom half of the wage distribution in many countries, including the US, since the 1980s. In the pre-democratic world of the early nineteenth century it was possible to suppress dissent but it is worth imagining the public response today were any policy maker to advocate rapid technological change while admitting most people would fail to benefit for over two generations.

A

Bach der Gonfiscation zweite Ausgabe.

A A poster calling for universal male suffrage and an eight-hour working day on Labour Day (also known as International Workers' Day), 1 May 1894.
B Trade union members march in Denmark and Australia on 1 May 1912 and 1913, demanding the legal adoption of an eight-hour working day. The campaign was initiated by the Second International, an organization of socialist and labour parties formed in 1889.

The **trade union movement** in the UK, which rose from around 1.5 million people in 1892 to over 8 million in 1919–20, reached its peak in 1979 with more than 13 million members. It then declined, before stabilizing somewhat in the mid 1990s.

B

In his influential book *The Great Transformation*, the Austrian Hungarian economic historian Karl Polyani (1886–1964) developed the concept of 'the double movement' to describe the process whereby economic and social upheaval wrought by capitalism and resulting in greater inequality leads to a counter reaction by and on behalf of the working class. The second half of the nineteenth century and early years of the twentieth saw a variety of responses to the working and living conditions resulting from industrialization. These included the growth of the trade union movement and of communist, socialist and social democratic parties committed to governing in the interest of the newly enfranchised working class.

This period also saw the beginnings of the state regulation of labour practices and the first steps towards forms of work-related welfare such as sickness and unemployment insurance. There were also some moves among reformers and paternalistic employers to explore more benign forms of employment.

Quakers, also known as Friends, value all people equally, believing that there is God in everyone. An historically Christian denomination, there are about 210,000 Quakers across the world.

A   Labour notes issued by the National Equitable labour Exchange, founded in 1932 by Robert Owen. Workers could exchange products they had made with labour notes representing the hours it had taken to make them.

B   Amenities for workers at Rowntree's factory in York and the Cadbury factory at Bournville model village included leisure, health care and education. Both companies were founded by Quakers.

A

Earliest and most pioneering among these was the New Lanark experiment instigated by Robert Owen (1771–1858), the principles of which Owen subsequently applied to the short-lived communal experiment of New Harmony in Indiana, USA. Owen was inspired by utopian socialism, but other reformers were motivated by faith. These included Quaker firms, among the most high profile being the confectionary empires of the Cadbury and Rowntree families and the Lever brothers who built the model community Port Sunlight in Merseyside, UK. In seeking not only to improve working conditions, but also to provide for the housing, leisure and educational needs of workers, the Victorian philanthropists manifested a paternalistic sense of duty, which has been a recurring, if occasional, aspect of the attitude of some labour owners and managers.

While the inspiration for compassion and generosity may have been religious or political conviction, there was also an element of enlightened self-interest; well cared for workers are likely to be more productive. Indeed, the first articulation of this argument may have been in the work of the Roman agriculture expert Lucius Columella (AD 4 – c. 70), who in the first century AD not only urged slave owners to treat their human possessions with care but even suggested consulting with them on domestic and working arrangements.

B

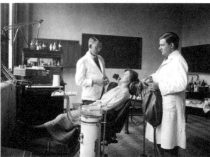

A

A   Panorama of the Bethleham Steel Works, Pennsylvania, c. 1912. This was the site for Frederick W. Taylor's research into working practices, research that laid the basis for Taylor's hugely influential theory of 'scientific management'.

The early twentieth century saw a new contribution to the debate about the use of sticks and carrots to motivate workers. The ideas of Frederick W. Taylor (1856–1915) were summed up in his 1911 monograph *The Principles of Scientific Management*, arguably the single most influential document in the modern history of labour relations. Taylor's principles were based on his observations of employees in various settings, including Bethlehem Steel Works in Pennsylvania. They led him to conclude that many workers were able deliberately to slow down their work rate, partly to protect jobs that they feared might be lost if productivity was higher.

Frederick W. Taylor was an American mechanical engineer and is thought by many to have been the first management consultant.

Henry Ford was an industrialist and business magnet. He founded the Ford Motor Company and his Model T Ford revolutionized both the production and consumption of cars.

In summary, Taylor's principles for managers, which were widely adopted and applied in industry, most notably by Henry Ford (1863–1947), are:

1. Develop a science for each element of a man's work.

2. Scientifically select and then train, teach and develop the workman.

3. Collaborate with the workmen to ensure all the work being done is in accordance with the principles of the science which has been developed.

4. The management take over all work for which they are better fitted than the workmen.

A   Lobbycard for Charlie Chaplin's film *Modern Times*, 1936. The film was a commentary on the tyranny of technology, and the struggle to preserve humanity in a mechanized world.

B   Assembly-line workers in a Ford Motor Company plant, Detroit, Michigan, 1913. Assembly-line work is monotonous. To reduce the high turnover of workers, in 1914 Ford raised wages to a then-unheard of $5 per day, against a norm of $2.25.

C   Assembly-line workers in a Ford factory in Dearborn, Michigan. By 1918, half of all cars in America were Ford Model Ts, also known as 'Tin Lizzies'.

Taylor's view that the antagonism between workers and managers could be overcome to the benefit of the enterprise by the right techniques and forms of engagement helped lay the foundations for personnel management (more often now called human resource management). However, while Taylor emphasized that his principles must be implemented together, in practice the core message taken by employers was the benefit of closely specified and mechanically enabled control over workflow.

This was a key moment in the debate about the relationship between technology, productivity and control at work which continues to this day, for example in debates about the use of AI-enabled surveillance to monitor and assess workers. With the rise of home working due to the COVID restrictions came allegations of employers finding digital methods to check their employees were focusing on their duties.

Henry Ford was one of Taylor's disciples but his business genius lay in the combination of scientific management with a model of high productivity, mass production consumerism. Ford paid his workers enough to be able to buy the cars they produced on the assembly line. Crucially, this cements an instrumental view of work in which its purpose is not dignity or fulfilment for workers but greater productivity leading to higher wages, leading to more scope for consumption.

Ford famously quipped that his cars came in any colour as long as it was black. Now car purchasers can choose from a huge and continuously changing variety of models. The expensive habit of regularly buying a new car has been cited by behavioural economists as an example of consumer irrationality as the pleasure of the purchase is short-lived. Henry Ford kickstarted the hedonic treadmill and it has been accelerating ever since.

Human resource management is the hiring, management and firing of employees – aiming to motivate and develop them and maximize performance in service of an organization's strategy.

AI-enabled surveillance tools, such as office sensors, algorithms and phone apps, can be used to generate real-time diagnoses of employees' health and wellbeing, productivity and risk-levels.

B

C

Labour markets go through cycles and trends and it is not always easy to distinguish between them. The public have tended to see the primary responsibility of government in relation to work as being to ensure sufficient jobs. The twentieth and early twenty-first century have seen significant periods of high unemployment, particularly in the 1930s depression. The 1970s and 1980s saw a rapid decline in manufacturing jobs resulting from both technological change and an increase in the share of goods produced by industrializing countries like South Korea and China.

A

B

C

A Workers on a jeep factory assembly line. There are an estimated 2,000 car makers in the world, although the bulk of car manufacturing is now owned by 14 major global companies.

B A worker uses a lathe in a mechanical factory in Shanghai, 1971. By the 1980s in China, around 11% of the workforce was employed by state-owned enterprises in the industrial sector.

C Stacked shelves of food at the Super Giant supermarket in Maryville, USA, 1964. As manufacturing work has declined in advanced economies, the service sector, for example, retail, has grown.

Behind the cycles have been significant shifts in the nature and context of employment in industrialized countries. There has been a major move in employment from primary sectors, including farming, fishing and mining, and secondary, principally manufacturing, to the service sector, ranging from public services like health and education to retail and hospitality. Today in an economy like the UK more than four in five workers are in the service sector. Connected to this shift in the content of work has been the rise in women's employment.

Women were encouraged to enter the workplace en masse during the First and Second World Wars, something which also contributed to the decline of domestic service which had been the largest single occupational category for women in the nineteenth century. After the wars most women were expected to withdraw from the labour market. The idea that the income from the male breadwinner should be sufficient to sustain a family and improve living standards was an assumption underlying business strategy, trade union demands and public policy during the period of the post-war settlement.

In the 1960s the UK participation rate of working age women was only a little more than half that of men, but by 2019 the gap was down to less than ten percentage points and closing. In many countries, the 1960s saw the first legislative action on gender pay disparities, including the American Equal Pay Act signed by President Kennedy (1917–1963) in 1963. This was the first step towards the much more comprehensive employment equalities legislation which exists in most nations. Although women are now almost as likely to be in paid work as men, they still bare most of the burden of the unpaid life-labour of sustaining home and family.

A

B

A An American female war work poster from the Second World War. The encouragement to women to work during the world wars was intended to be temporary, and although many were demoted or left after the war ended, the policy led to lasting changes in the workforce.

B The international Wages for Housework Campaign issued this poster in 1976, demanding payment for all domestic work and childcare.

C Vintage 1970s Women's Liberation Movement badges. Among the demands of the movement were equal opportunities and pay in the workplace.

c

The **post-war settlement** lasted from the end of the Second World War until the election of Margaret Thatcher in 1979. It was characterized by a mixed economy and the creation of the welfare state, low unemployment, economic growth and rising living standards.

Along with the move to services and the growth of female participation, a third twentieth-century shift is particularly relevant to current debates about work. Following the economic and political polarization of the 1930s, and reflecting the need for reconstruction, the architects of the post-war settlement emphasized social solidarity and industrial partnership. This was an era of relatively low levels of inequality, of expanding welfare provision, and strong government working alongside business associations and trade unions.

The **oil crisis of the 1970s** was caused by OPEC (Organization of the Petroleum Exporting Countries) embargoing oil sales to the USA, in retaliation for US support to the Israeli military during the Yom Kippur War. It contributed to stagflation and economic downturns during the decade.

In a **zero-hours contract** the employer does not provide a minimum number of working hours to the employee. Some workers find the flexibility beneficial, but they contribute to precariousness and give firms the power to deny work to those who are non-compliant.

In **gig work** the worker is paid while they are undertaking a task rather than for contracted hours. It is often associated with internet platforms such Uber and Deliveroo.

A

Following the oil crisis of the 1970s, several connected factors contributed to a new era. These including shifts in the labour market and the associated decline of trade union membership and strength, but also the increasing importance of educational attainment in employment outcomes, and the acceleration of globalization and financialization. Exacerbating the impact of these factors was a neo-liberal ideology which favoured market deregulation and minimizing the role of the state and other non-market institutions.

As a result inequality rose in most Western nations, the living standards of those in the bottom half of the income distribution stagnated and new phenomena emerged such as high levels of in-work poverty and an increase in various forms of precarious employment of which zero-hours contracts and gig work are the most controversial.

As Karl Polyani would have predicted, the neoliberal turn has led to a counter reaction. Greater public awareness during the COVID-19 crisis of the plight of precarious workers, and the value of 'key workers' – ranging from care assistants to delivery drivers – are part of more general sense that the shift in economic outcomes and power away from ordinary working people has gone too far. One sign of that turn was the appointment in 2017 by the then UK Prime Minister Theresa May of this book's author to lead an inquiry into modern employment practices. In my report I called for good work for all. But what is good work and how far from it are we?

3. The Discontents of Work

Centre for Better Ageing is a charity to research and advocate for better lives for older citizens. It is part of the UK government's network of What Works Centres.

A

The Japanese concept of *ikigai* can be roughly defined as 'reason for being'. It is often portrayed visually as the central zone created by four overlapping circles respectively representing; 'what you are good at', 'what you love', 'what you can be paid for' and 'what the world needs'. It is the experience of work most of us would like but few of us attain.

How far most workers are from reaching such a state of eudemonic wellbeing was captured by a 2105 opinion poll about retirement conducted by the Centre for Better Ageing. When older workers were asked what they would miss about their jobs, the most common answer by some distance was 'nothing at all'. Why does so much work fall short of *ikigai* and why do we put up with it? It has always been the case that some types of work have been seen as less desirable than others. Yet it is significant that variations in job satisfaction between occupations are generally smaller than those between contented and discontented people in similar types of work. Beyond a certain minimum level, pay differences are also a relatively small factor.

As we will explore in the next chapter, there are ways to make all jobs feel more fulfilling and valued. Job satisfaction has a subjective element and reflects people's personal and non-work priorities. Overall, though, good work may be less about the content of jobs and more about the power relations and assumptions that underpin employment. What are the generic factors that make work feel unfair or dissatisfying? Three 'c's stand out; control, competition and consumerism.

A A school teacher and students in Sri Lanka: good work is rewarding for workers and for society.

B Hairdressing salons in Barcelona, Spain, and in Brazil. Hairdressing has been a fast-growing form of employment in many countries. While the work is often low paid, surveys have found hairdressers to be amongst the most contented workers, partly because of the sense of providing satisfaction to customers.

Control flows from ownership and the power that comes with it. From obeying the law to following the rules and advice set by a wide range of institutions we encounter in our day-to-day life, we all spend a lot of time doing what we are told to. Sometimes authority is imposed by force but more often we accept it. The question may be less 'why do some people give orders' and more 'why do most of us obey them'. The answer according to German sociologist Max Weber (1864–1920) lies in forms of legitimation. Contrasting it with the 'traditional' and 'charismatic' legitimacy of the pre-industrial world, Weber described the basis of authority in the modern world as being 'rational-legal'. This type of legitimacy has various forms.

A

INDEX OF SELF-EMPLOYMENT AS A PROPORTION OF TOTAL EMPLOYMENT (2003=100)
(2003–2018)

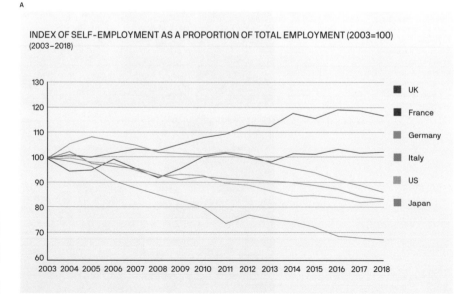

■ UK
■ France
■ Germany
■ Italy
■ US
■ Japan

A This graph from the Institute of Employment Studies shows the steady increase in self-employment in the UK and a small increase in France, whereas in other countries there has been a fall. The relatively higher numbers of people who want to 'be their own boss' in the UK and France may suggest a greater resistance to managerial control.

B Boardroom executives in London look out at students protesting against the trebling of tuition fees, November 2011. in the vast majority of medium and large organizations decision-making power lies in the hands of boards whose primary role is generally seen to be representing the interests of owners.

B

Political authority is based on democracy and the rule of law. Expert authority rests in a belief in objectivity and a respect for scientific method and reputation. It is noteworthy that both these forms have been under attack with the rise of populism. But it is the third form of rational-legal legitimacy that is the most relevant to the discussion of work; ownership.

Despite the rise of self-employment in some countries, including the UK, in recent decades, in most developed nations over four in five workers are employed by someone else. The authority relationship explicit in the employment contract and implicit in day to day management is ultimately based on the ownership of an enterprise. This is also true of public services and non-profit organizations where accountable officers or Boards of Trustees will act as custodians of the organization and its resources.

A

A   The Grunwick dispute, London, 1976. Bad employment practices can become a national issue as in this dispute, which saw national trade union mobilization behind the demand for union recognition among the mainly female Asian workforce of a north London factory.

B   Unions gathering in solidarity with striking employees at an Amazon plant in Naples, Italy, 2021. Warehouse workers in many countries are on casual contracts denying them full employment rights.

C   Workers fulfil orders among shelves lined with goods at an Amazon warehouse in Brieselang, Germany, 2015. Work such as picking and packing in warehouses – often on zero-hours contracts – usually lacks the basic components of good work, including autonomy, the scope to progress and rights to representation and consultation.

The imbalance in power between the owners of organizations and their agents, on the one hand, and those who are hired by them, on the other, is central to radical critiques of capitalist society and to the policy programmes of reformers. As we saw in the last chapter, the response to the oppression and immiseration of early industrialization involved steps to mitigate this power imbalance.

Modern employers face a wide range of responsibilities – from health and safety measures to equality legislation – which constrain the arbitrary use of the power flowing from ownership. Equally, employees have a set of entitlements and rights which address their lack of ownership stakes in the workplace. Good employers may offer a number of additional benefits, including for example the opportunity to work from home, something which, of course, expanded hugely during the COVID pandemic.

Nevertheless, the reality, particularly for those in poorer paid, lower quality employment with less market power, can be intensive, wide-ranging and sometimes arbitrary authority. Furthermore, many employers have expanded the use of forms of casual employment such as zero-hours contracts or gig work as a way of maximizing their flexibility and minimizing their responsibilities. Although in countries such as the UK and US there is a public appetite for enhanced legal protection for precarious workers, large-scale unemployment of the kind that is likely in the wake of COVID will significantly weaken the bargaining power of workers.

Health and safety regulation has increased from the 1833 Factory Acts, limiting child labour, to recent rules about social distancing to avoid the spread of COVID in the workplace. A popular phrase among those pointing to what they see as excessive protections is 'health and safety gone mad'.

The American philosopher Elizabeth Anderson has referred to the business employment relationship as 'private government'. Anderson's argument is that employers are granted power over employees at work in a way that is analogous to the power the state has over citizens. However, while those with democratic authority are subject to accountability and being removed from office by citizens, the only way for workers to escape unresponsive authority is to resign, something which may be very disadvantageous or risky for them.

Anderson's focus is on the US. Many countries – especially in western and northern Europe – have a more expansive framework of protection and rights, including mechanisms to provide workers a say at work, such as the Works Councils in German firms, which were first established in the 1920s.

A   Discussions on the adoption of the first German Works Councils Act in the Reichstag, 1920. European Union regulations require that all workers have rights to information, consultation and representation.

B   Traders in Seoul, South Korea, 2020. Companies must compete in the market for consumers and investment. But is competitive success alone a sufficient basis for work satisfaction?

C   Traders on the floor of the New York Stock Exchange, 2018. Firms compete for investment from shareholders by promising strong returns and offering generous dividends.

A

A **Works Council** is a form of industrial partnership (particularly associated with Germany) in which an employer has a supervisory board made up substantially of employee representatives.

B

C

Yet, surveys of employee satisfaction consistently find that the quality of relationship workers have with their managers is a critical factor. One way to make work feel more like something we choose and that fulfils us, rather than just paying our bills, would be to reduce the power imbalance between employers and employees and, where authority is necessary, to see it exercised in benign and enlightened ways.

Of course, managers also complain that they have limited autonomy. This may be connected to a second factor standing in the way of better work; the ethic of competition. Competition is an important source of dynamism in any system, but particularly in a capitalist economy. The value and resilience of nations, places, organizations and individuals is often measured in terms of their ability to vie with their peers. As well as competing for market share, the pursuit of maximum profitability is also driven by competition for financial investment.

A

B

Comparative advantage
describes an economy's ability to produce a product at a lower opportunity cost than those it trades with. Such an advantage enables a company to sell goods and services more cheaply and to make larger margins.

New Public Management
was developed by academics and consultants in Australia, the USA and UK in the 1980s. The aim of NPM was to make government more business-like, thereby addressing perceived failings, such as inefficiency, unresponsiveness and 'producer capture'.

Competition can drive better performance and greater innovation and provides the mechanism for maximizing comparative advantage. It can also provide an efficient mechanism for accountability, exposing those who are under-performing or are making profit without adding value, what economists call 'rent-seeking'. Competition is not only extolled by the ideological champions of free market capitalism; progressives seek to reign in the power of major corporations – like the tech giants – which are able to exercise monopolistic control of markets.

From national policy to the practices of individual organizations, the pursuit of competitiveness has often been a rationale for intensifying work and minimizing rewards and entitlements for workers.

The de-regulatory, anti-trade union policies pursued by New Right leaders Ronald Reagan (1911–2004) and Margaret Thatcher (1925–2013) were justified in part by the need to compete with rising economies like South Korea and Japan. Social democratic leaders like Tony Blair (b. 1953) in the UK and Gerhard Schroeder (b. 1944) in Germany adopted a more balanced approach, but still accepted the underlying logic of competitive globalization. While the competitive spirit is particularly strong in the private sector, New Public Management, the school of thought that dominated thinking about government services from the 1980s until recently, drove quasi-markets to the public and third sectors, and thus extended the logic of competition across all forms of employment, including care.

When competition is the overriding priority, everything else, including the treatment of workers, tends to take a back seat. One example came in the summer of 2020. A spike in COVID-19 infections in Leicester in the English East Midlands, combined with undercover work by journalists, laid bare widespread labour abuses in the city's extensive garment industry. This included people working long hours for well below the statutory minimum wage in dangerous conditions without any genuine effort to observe social distancing.

C

A Margaret Thatcher and Ronald Reagan, pictured here together on the White House lawn in 1985, were standard bearers for the free market, minimal state policies of neo-liberalism.

B *Spitting Image* puppets of Thatcher and Reagan, 1985. Although widely satirized, both figures were electorally successful and their ideas became dominant.

C Workers in Leicester's garment industry. Businesses such as this were exposed in 2020 for non-payment of the national minimum wage, VAT fraud and inadequate health and safety.

The problems in Leicester had been an
open secret for many years, exacerbated
by the limited powers of enforcement agencies
and the unwillingness of victims to report
issues. But one of the key drivers is the ultra-
competitive nature of the fast fashion industry.
Consumers have got used to extremely cheap
clothes and continuously changing styles.
These are delivered by an industry in which
already tight margins at the top of the labour
supply chain are then subcontracted to the
point at which only those employers willing
to circumvent rules and employees willing to
accept illegal conditions are able to get work.

Although major brands – like
Boohoo – denied they used
sweatshop labour, an independent
QC-led inquiry set up by the firm
revealed a considerable degree
of complicity. But responsibility
extends further; despite Boohoo
and its sub-brands being subject
to extensive negative publicity
there was little evidence of an
impact on sales.

A

A	Advertising billboards for Boohoo and Pretty Little Thing, a Boohoo brand, at Canary Wharf station, London, 2018. Fast-fashion retailer Boohoo includes several popular brands, including Karen Millen, Coast, Oasis and Warehouse. Despite adverse publicity about the treatment of its workers, sales and profits surged during the COVID period.

B	Workers operate sewing machines in a garment factory in Solo, Java, 2019. The business model of fast fashion involves just-in-time manufacture of cheap garments by low-paid workers to respond immediately to changing customer preferences.

C	One of the by-products of the fast-fashion industry has been a huge increase in discarded textiles, many of which end up in landfill sites such as this.

B

C

A single-minded focus on competition can impact in other ways. Max Weber saw the process of rationalization, through which more and more areas of society are subject to calculation, as a defining characteristic of the modern age. Weber drew a distinction between 'substantive' rationality directed to the ultimate human ends of actions and 'formal' rationality focused on the means of achieving those ends. For example, the ends of a criminal trial are to establish the truth, exonerate the innocent and prosecute the guilty, but the means are the rules covering issues like use of evidence or court procedure. Weber argued that in organizations run on a rationalistic basis (which Weber saw as the key characteristic of bureaucracy), the formal rationality of means and rules tends to obscure the substantive rationality of human outcomes.

A

At our best, human beings are driven by intrinsic motivations connected to fulfilling our potential as unique individuals and as members of society. Surveys show that a sense of purpose, both in our own work and the wider aims and impact of our employer or hirer, is an important component of job satisfaction and wellbeing. Competitive motivation can help achieve substantive progress but only if that which is being competed over is ultimately of value. When it seems that all that drives us is competition, and when the aim of competing is something the worth of which is opaque or contested – such as market share, a position in a performance league table or stock market price – the culture of that organization and the work within is likely to be inherently dehumanizing.

As the economist and journalist John Kay – who has argued strongly for companies to focus on ultimate purpose – has written: 'No one will be buried with the epitaph "He maximized shareholder value".' Competitive quasi-markets in public services have been associated with doctors and teachers displacing ethical and professional goals by playing the system to meet targets such as for maximum waiting times or for children reaching a certain attainment threshold.

A   Firms seek to motivate staff through bonuses or awards such as 'Employee of the month' or 'Outstanding employee'. However, for many workers, whether their employer's activities have social value is also important.

B   Yale University campus shop. League tables of performance have proliferated in sectors such as higher education, as every student shops around and institutions compete to prove they are best at something.

C   Stanford University merchandizing. The commodification of education was underlined in 2019 when several rich and famous parents were found to have been bribing their children's way into elite colleges.

The **shareholder value** of a firm is based on the money generated to equity holders in the form of dividends and capital growth. The phrase is also associated with the principle that maximizing the share prices should be the primary goal of company directors and executives.

Feeling part of a team is one of the most often quoted aspects of job satisfaction. But here again the imperatives of competition have an impact. In the post-war period, echoing aspects of nineteenth-century paternalism, many large companies invested in social and leisure facilities for staff. Under pressure from investors and the threat of hostile takeover much of this has been stripped back, with the company playing fields that used to be common in city suburbs long since sold off. More perniciously, competition forces divisions within staff as they vie for bonuses or promotion. While elements of this may be inevitable in any hierarchy, divide and rule is often a deliberate management tactic.

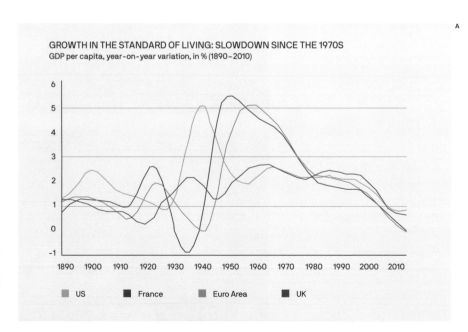

GROWTH IN THE STANDARD OF LIVING: SLOWDOWN SINCE THE 1970S
GDP per capita, year-on-year variation, in % (1890–2010)

■ US   ■ France   ■ Euro Area   ■ UK

Performance-related pay is a widespread system in which employees are rewarded according to how they perform in relation to specified targets. The systems are often based on comparisons between staff, meaning better pay relies on being able to outperform colleagues.

A   This graph shows that the growth in the economic standard of living accelerated in the first half of the 20th century but has slowed in the USA and Europe since the 1970s mainly due to a reduction in productivity.

B   In the 19th and 20th centuries many large companies provided extensive sports facilities for staff and their families. Pictured here are the families of employees during the 1950s playing football at the sports ground and enjoying the swimming pool belonging to the London brick company Stewartby.

For example, a report into the culture of retail banking set up after a pension mis-selling scandal in which millions of UK citizens were persuaded to buy inappropriate products described how one bank held a weekly 'cash or cabbages' ritual in which people with strong sales figures got money while low performers were presented with the unloved vegetable. Performance-related pay is widely used as a management tool although research suggests it is counter-productive for complex tasks involving the use of cognitive skills.

Those harassed bank staff were no doubt told they were in a fight to the death for customers with other pension providers. The power of consumerism is another reason we tolerate unfulfilling work. Despite a stagnation in working-class incomes in recent decades, technological advance has enabled a transformation in the standard of life and opportunities available to the citizens of developed countries. For most of human existence people have worked in order primarily to survive and reproduce. Today we work to pay for everything from HD televisions to foreign holidays, from haircuts to massages.

A

Puritanism was a religious movement that began in England in the late 16th century. Like Calvinism, it was deeply hostile to Catholicism. In 1620 the *Mayflower*, carrying 102 English Puritan emigrants, landed at Cape Cod, America.

As we saw, the idea of the dignity of labour has roots in early Christianity teaching, but Max Weber and other thinkers including R. H. Tawney (1880–1962) saw the rise of capitalism as enabled by the religious values of Protestantism and Puritanism, which put an emphasis on hard work, self-help and deferred gratification. Henry Ford developed a different way of thinking about motivating working people; not compulsion, mere subsistence or a reward in heaven, but the bounteous possibilities of shopping. From the idea of an affordable family car, consumerism has grown to be the driving force in developed world economies and central to the identity of modern citizens.

Two processes have intersected to shift our identity. Factors such as the decline of traditional industries, the abandonment by most big businesses of social, cultural and sporting activities for workers and the rise of precarious forms of employment have lessened our sense of identity as workers.

At the same time marketing, now accelerated by social media, has reinforced our identity as consumers. The idea that we are defined by how we spend money as much, if not more than, by how we earn it reinforces an instrumental account of the value of work. The daily grind might not offer succour to the soul or a sense of belonging but that can be found in the house you live in, what you wear and how you spend your leisure time.

A 2013 essay titled 'On the phenomenon of bullshit jobs' by American anthropologist and anti-globalization campaigner David Greaber (1961–2020) went viral globally and led to a book version. Greaber's examples of people who considered their jobs worthless included a friend who had become a successful New York corporate lawyer. A subsequent YouGov poll found that more than a third of UK workers found their employment 'meaningless', but very few said they were intending to leave their jobs; after all they have stuff to buy and bills to pay.

A   Shoppers on a Black Friday sales day in São Paulo, Brazil, 2018. Our identity as a consumer is for many people more important than that as a worker.

B   The internet and social media have intensified consumerism. If successful, these Italian TikTok influencers will use their fame to promote products to their followers.

C   A livestreaming event in a Shanghai studio. Livestream shopping – in which influencers sell products to their followers – is a nearly $70 billion industry in China alone.

A Social media consumerism exemplified by Instagram's checkout feature.

B Producers need to comply with strict guidelines in order to be able to label a product 'organic'. Such a label ensures appeal to consumers concerned with environmental issues and guarantees a higher price point.

C Retailers selling mass-produced goods often try to persuade customers of their authenticity by using terms like 'traditional'.

D A bottle of 'hand-made' Tito's vodka. In 2015 its makers were sued in the US for wrongful use of the term given the company's automated production process but, despite settling out of court, the brand remains unchanged.

In the 1960s and 70s the American sociologist Daniel Bell (1919–2011) wrote extensively on **post-industrial society**. In his influential book *The Cultural Contradictions of Capitalism* (1976), he highlighted the difference between the demands of productive capitalism – including diligence and patience – with those of consumerism – instant gratification. Bell believed consumer values were making society weaker and less governable. A hundred years before Bell, Karl Marx identified the alienation experienced by workers as they lose control over their work process and the intrinsic 'use value' of their labour was relegated behind its 'exchange value' for business owners and consumers.

A

B   C   D

When we think of the value and authenticity of an artefact, our knowledge of its maker and the process of its creation is often an element; we are interested in how it was made, who made it and what motivated them. Recognizing this, consumer brands are fond of spuriously using phrases like 'hand made', 'locally produced' or 'family run' which acknowledge a yearning to connect to how things are produced. Yet, for busy consumers the manner of production is generally secondary to considerations of taste and price. Often – as in the case of fast fashion – it seems we would rather not have to think about the plight of the workers. Internet shopping, which encourages fast choices and ranking by price, tends to further narrow our focus.

AL PACINO JACK LEMMON ALEC BALDWIN ED HARRIS ALAN ARKIN KEVIN SPACEY JONATHAN PRYCE

A Story For Everyone Who Works For A Living.

GLENGARRY GLEN ROSS

A

Pension mis-selling takes place when a customer is prevailed upon to buy or sell a pension when it is not in their interests by a vendor or advisor who could reasonably be expected to know this.

Economic insecurity describes the risk of economic hardship faced by workers and households as they encounter unpredictable events such as sickness, loss of work or the need to replace an essential item, such as a car or washing machine.

A   A 1992 poster for the film version of David Mamet's play *Glengarry Glen Ross* (1984). It is one of many depictions in popular culture of salesmen as desperate, ruthless and cut-throat.

B   The growth of high-interest, short-term, no questions asked, pay-day loan providers is one sign of economic insecurity and the growth of people with poor credit ratings.

Conversely, workers can be required by their bosses to exploit consumers. Examples like pension mis-selling, show how a whole group of workers can be embroiled in persuading people like themselves to act against their own interest. In his book *To Sell is Human* (2012), the best-selling American author Daniel H. Pink argues that most jobs in the modern economy involve some form of selling. Yet, in common parlance the idea of being a 'salesman' or offering a 'sales pitch' is often associated with insincerity and attempted manipulation. Most of us are both workers and shoppers. The hard sell of consumerism can pitch the two sides of our identity against each other.

Consumerism has made life more pleasant and less effortful in many ways, but by continually generating new needs it also creates new pressures and stresses.

One side-effect of a culture of instant gratification, combined with financial deregulation, has been the growth of credit. Personal debt levels in the UK and US have grown to huge levels. This contributes to the rise of economic insecurity. An RSA survey in 2017 found that four in ten people said their finances were precarious while three in ten said they were not managing. Significantly, insecurity does not impact the poor alone. Those who suffer can be on relatively high incomes but simply spending more than they can afford. Economic insecurity means people are more likely to feel they have no choice but to take a job or stay in a job which they do not like. It also increases people's sense of anxiety and powerlessness at work.

There are important aspects of our societies that define and limit work; the relationship between ownership and control, the emphasis on competitiveness for its own sake and the privileging of consumption as the expression of social progress and personal achievement. As a result, only a few people can truly say that employment, the main activity of most of our adult lives, is a source of growth and fulfilment. Perhaps it is time to change the question?

B

4. Good Work For All?

Between full-time education and retirement, paid work takes up around a third of our waking hours. It decisively influences the choices available to us and our quality of life. Yet the pattern of work in modern society is not the outcome of a debate about human potential and fulfilment. It is the result of historical contingency, economic expediency and the assumptions and interests of the powerful. What if, rather than having to adapt to the needs of the economy or the boss, the nature of work reflected our needs and potential?

A

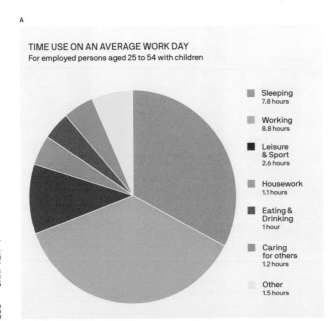

TIME USE ON AN AVERAGE WORK DAY
For employed persons aged 25 to 54 with children

Sleeping
7.8 hours

Working
8.8 hours

Leisure & Sport
2.6 hours

Housework
1.1 hours

Eating & Drinking
1 hour

Caring for others
1.2 hours

Other
1.5 hours

Key workers is a term generally applied to public service employees who provide essential services, such as health, education, policing and care. The term has also been used more widely to include other people working during lockdown, such as delivery drivers.

B

In several countries, before the COVID-19 pandemic, the case for better work had started to receive more public and political attention. In part this reflected the relative strength of labour markets; when the quantity of jobs is less of a concern, more attention can be paid to their quality. An aspiration for good work chimes with concerns about inequality and the demeaning and intensive conditions endured by, for example, zero-hours warehouse workers. It also featured in conversations among the public and policy makers about the potential impact of technology at work, although, as is often the case, speculation tended to focus more on the capabilities of machines than the preferences of people.

The COVID-19 pandemic has further strengthened public concern about precarious employment and raised awareness of the social significance of a variety of 'key workers'. With unemployment again a pressing issue in the wake of the post-COVID economic downturn, it may be more difficult to maintain a focus on quality of work. But the answer is to be more, not less, ambitious.

A

There have been various attempts to describe the contours of good work. A report by the Carnegie UK Trust and the RSA Future Work Centre based on academic research and employee surveys identified seven dimensions:

1. Terms of employment, including job security and guaranteed hours

2. Pay and benefits – not just level of pay but a sense that it is fair

3. Health, safety and psychosocial wellbeing

4. Job design and nature of work, including use of skills, level of control and sense of purpose

5. Social support and cohesion from colleagues and managers

6. Voice and representation

7. Work–life balance

The UK government is now committed to measuring and reporting on the quality of work.

Work quality matters for several reasons. In terms of social justice, the lowest paid jobs tend also to be the most unpleasant and with the fewest opportunities for growth or progression. People in bad work are more likely to suffer ill-health and to drop out of employment and on to welfare benefits. There is an economic argument too. Research suggests – unsurprisingly – that engaged employees are more productive. Indeed, at the higher end of the labour market, competing for scarce talent can lead companies to outbid each other not just in terms of pay but employee-friendly working arrangements.

A UBS staff gathering as part of the company's contribution to the charity Operation Santa Claus, 2016. A sense of teamwork and purpose are key elements of job satisfaction.
B A WeWork shared office space in China. Employers can offer a range of benefits beyond pay to attract staff. Such benefits are rarely on offer to lower paid, lower skilled or casual workers.
C Stuffed toy animals are displayed as part of social distancing measures in the dining area at rental office Spaces Shinagawa, Tokyo, Japan, 2020.

Psychosocial refers to the interconnectness of social and individual factors. For example a high pressure environment might contribute to individual anxiety and associated physical illness.

A   Edward L. Deci and Richard Ryan's self-determination theory is the foundation for much positive psychology. It identifies the desire for autonomy, mastery and connectedness as our three core intrinsic motivations.

If more jobs, particularly lower paid, lower skilled jobs, scored highly on the Carnegie/RSA seven dimensions fewer people would find work onerous. As we have seen, since the depredations of industrialization working conditions have improved over the long term. Incremental change has made a difference. Yet, the implicit starting point for the good work agenda is still to take the nature of work and society for granted while trying to improve what is possible within those parameters. A different and more radical starting point is not work as we currently think of it, but asking what human beings need to thrive.

One answer can be found in social psychology, with self-determination theory, which was developed from the 1970s by psychologists Edward L. Deci and Richard Ryan and is now the foundation for much positive psychology. The focus of their work was on people's intrinsic motivations; the needs we must fulfil to promote psychological health and wellbeing. Deci and Ryan argued that these drives are innate and universal. They identified three intrinsic motivations: 'autonomy', 'competence' and 'relatedness'. All human beings are inclined to try to fulfil these basic needs but social conditions shape whether they can do so.

A

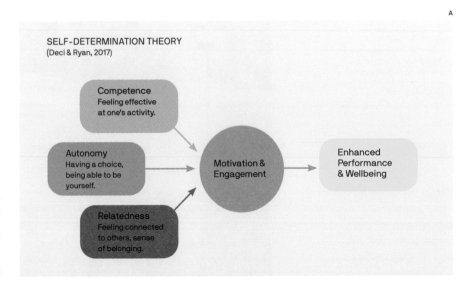

SELF-DETERMINATION THEORY
(Deci & Ryan, 2017)

Competence
Feeling effective at one's activity.

Autonomy
Having a choice, being able to be yourself.

Relatedness
Feeling connected to others, sense of belonging.

Motivation & Engagement

Enhanced Performance & Wellbeing

Positive psychology is a movement and set of ideas founded by Martin Seligman (b. 1942) in 1988. It seeks to address a traditional focus in psychology pathology and illness with exploration of the individual and social conditions for human flourishing.

'Crowding out' is a term first used by Swiss economist Bruno Frey (b. 1941) in 1997, but the idea was developed by influential British social researcher Richard Titmuss (1907–73) who argued – in the context of blood donations – that financial rewards reduce altruistic motivations, leading to unintended consequences.

With paid work in mind, it is significant that research has also found that extrinsic motivations like material rewards can 'crowd out' intrinsic ones. A famous example came from a research study of the behaviour of nursery school parents in Haifa in Israel published in 2000 by Aldo Rustichini and Uri Gneezy. In the attempt to encourage more parents to pick up their children on time, the nursery instituted fines. But the outcome was that more parents arrived late. Instead of being intrinsically motivated by a sense of responsibility to the institution, their children or the teachers, the parents started to see punctuality as a transactional commitment; the fine was not a token of disapproval but a fee in payment.

This helps to explain why performance-related pay often fails; instead of adding to motivation it replaces an intrinsic desire to do a good job with the extrinsic motivation of material reward, something that can lead employees to game the system or feel resentful if they do not get a bonus.

A

B

Universal Basic Income (UBI), payable unconditionally to every citizen, has been suggested by thinkers as diverse as radical activist Thomas Paine (1737–1809) and free-market economist Milton Friedman (1912–2006).

Means-tested benefits are lost when an individual's earning increases, creating a poverty trap whereby the low paid face a very high marginal income loss as they simultaneously lose benefits and start to pay tax.

How would work need to change to satisfy our intrinsic motivations? Let's start with autonomy. Could employment meet our need to be the causal agent in our own life, acting in line with our own beliefs and intentions?

One aspect might involve removing the financial necessity to take work. The idea of a Universal Basic Income (UBI) – a payment made by the state to every adult citizen to enable them at least to subsist – is sometimes portrayed as an antidote to work. This is a perspective that echoes the tendency of the ancients to see effortful work as belittling or the anarchist ideal contained in the title of an essay published in 1880 by Paul Lafargue (1842–1911), the Cuban born son-in-law of Karl Marx: 'The right to be lazy'.

However, more mainstream thinking about UBI, including real-world experiments, has a different purpose. On the one hand, the aim is to strengthen work incentives. Unlike means-tested benefits, UBI is not lost when someone starts to earn money. This means it can loosen the poverty trap. On the other hand, by unconditionally meeting basic income needs, UBI makes it more possible to try out a new life direction like training or trying to set up a business. Its existence might reduce the pressure on people to do unpleasant and unsatisfying work and be a broader cultural signal of an approach to work based less on necessity and more on choice. Research on the largest UBI experiment, recently conducted in Finland, finds that it boosts wellbeing while slightly strengthening incentives to work among most groups.

A UBI might give people more autonomy over whether and how to work but what about people's experience in work? As Deci and Ryan suggest, research finds a greater sense of autonomy at work is linked to wellbeing, although different aspects matter more to men and women, with the former focusing on work process and the latter on flexibility in hours and location. Despite these findings, work, particularly work that might be classified as semi- or low-skilled, is often designed to minimize autonomy.

A Grace, a retired villager in Kenya, is part of a trial of universal basic income by the NGO Give Directly, one of many pilot UBIs being tested aroud the world.

B A supporter carries a sign supporting Democratic presidential candidate Andrew Yang's plan for a $1,000 monthly universal basic income during a rally in Washington Square Park, New York, May 2019.

C Developed countries provide a range of 'active labour market' services to help people get back into work, such as the French agency *Pole Emploi*.

D An employment office in Novosibirsk, Russia. Services such as this combine assessing entitlement to benefits with employment support.

A

Holacracy is a decentralized organizational approach to management and governance. The key structural unit in holacracies is self-organizing teams rather than a managerial hierarchy. Forms of holacracy have been adopted by businesses and charities in a several countries.

As we saw, this was the assumption underlying F. W. Taylor's principles of scientific management and his advocacy of time and motion studies; if there is one best, most productive, way of doing things then workers should have no choice but to work this way, however mind numbing and soul destroying it might be.

A radically different way of approaching work design was described in the 2014 book *Reinventing Organizations* by the Belgian management theorist Frederic Laloux. Laloux's approach is based on the ideas of evolutionary human development derived from the integral theory developed by various thinkers including American philosopher Ken Wilbur. Indeed, what makes Laloux's analysis particularly interesting is that he starts not with work as it is, but with a broader theory of human nature and growth.

A An example of a time and motion study from 1947, highlighting the various ways in which efficiency is hampered by poor layout of parts and tools. Although autonomy is a core intrinsic motivation the aim of approaches like this is to minimize worker discretion.

B The holacracy model developed by Brian Robertson is one of number of attempts to explore alternative organizational models to the traditional hierarchical pyramid.

Laloux describes a range of organizations – from small radical collectives to one of the largest American tomato processing businesses – which have adopted a radically decentralized, trust-based organizational form.

One such company is the domiciliary health care company Buurtzorg. It was established in 2006 by Jos de Blok, provides a large proportion of Dutch home care and is being replicated in several other parts of the world. The Buurtzorg model is based on decentralizing the organization and provision of care to small self-managing groups of nurses. These teams in turn provide a flexible service to patients and their families, aiming to combine professional health care support with the contribution of patients, families, friends and communities. Buurtzorg consistently achieves high satisfaction ratings from both staff and patients and has the same costs as more traditional, top-down systems. Similar principles of decentralization, empowerment and trust underpin holacracy, developed in 2007 by Brian Robertson, founder of the tech company Ternary Software and most famously implemented by the online clothing and shoe retailer Zappos.

B

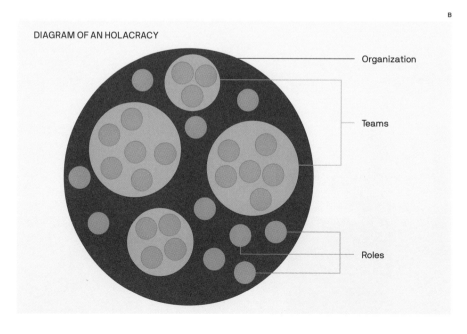

DIAGRAM OF AN HOLACRACY

Organization

Teams

Roles

Running organizations on these principles is not easy, but it can work. Buurtzorg and Zappos have been influential examples and others may follow in their footsteps. The history of work organization shows that a handful of pioneers can shape practice widely.

In terms of Deci and Ryan's second motivation, 'relatedness', teamwork is an important part of radically decentralized approaches, replacing top-down control with peer-to-peer support and encouragement. Unlike competitive regimes, the ethos is of collaboration and trust. Our colleagues are a major reason why we enjoy work but a survey in 2018 found that most UK office workers feel lonely.

A

A Desk workers in Ottawa, Canada, 2012. Loneliness at work became a big issue during the COVID lockdowns but research has also found that many workers feel lonely in the office.
B Working from home in San Francisco, September 2020. Home working increased dramatically during the COVID pandemic.
C Working from home in London, March 2020. Many employees want to continue home working after the pandemic.

B

C

Industrial democracy refers to workers having a stake in management, policy making and ownership of the enterprise in which they are employed. The term can be used to cover arrangements ranging from worker ownership to mandatory consultation.

The importance of connection may be why, as COVID reduction measures stretched into the autumn and winter of 2020, many workers started to talk about the impact on their wellbeing of working from home. The flexibility and time and money saved on commuting did not compensate for the loss of human contact.

Another possible way to strengthen both collective autonomy and relatedness lies in forms of industrial democracy, such as the German Works Councils and similar forms in other countries. These models do not change the ownership structure of enterprises, but they moderate the relationship between ownership and control by giving workers rights to be consulted and engaged.

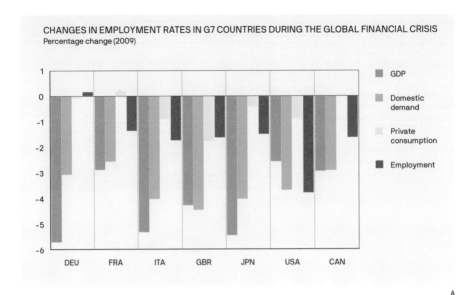

GDP

Domestic demand

Private consumption

Employment

DEU FRA ITA GBR JPN USA CAN

A

It is notable that Germany, which has arguably the longest and most deeply established model, has not only benefited from high productivity but also relatively harmonious industrial relations, generous employee terms and benefits (including flexible and falling working hours) and also a capacity to respond in innovative and fair ways to disruptions such as the global financial crisis and COVID-19.

For example the Kurzarbeit system agreed with employers and employee organizations enables enterprises to cut working hours and thereby reduce costs and the need for redundancies while the government helps compensate employees for the resulting loss of earnings. Many countries – including the UK – implemented their own versions of Kurzarbeit during the COVID crisis.

The **Kurzarbeit system** allows businesses to reduce workers' hours and apply to the government to have their wages subsidized. The chart (A) shows how it helped protect jobs after the global financial crisis of 2008.

A sense of **purpose**, rather than targets unrelated to doing good in the world, has been suggested by researchers to not only make organizations more productive, but also make them more attractive to potential recruits.

Environmental, social and corporate governance (ESG) is the term applied to the key factors determining the wider impact of business investment and activity. ESG has spawned a major industry of consultants and researchers.

B-Corporations, through which organizations must provide information to demonstrate commitment across a set of ethical, social and environmental measures, is a fast-growing initiative.

A This bar chart shows that after the 2008 financial crisis, Germay stood out among the G7 countries for keeping employment stable. Many firms in Germany negotiated shorter working weeks with employee representatives on Works Councils, thus reducing the need for redundancies.

B A variety of B-Corporation certificates from around the world.

The sense of relatedness at work – that workers are involved in a common endeavour – can be fostered by a stronger focus on purpose. This can help mitigate the organizational problem described by Max Weber of the substantive rationality of ultimate ends being squeezed out by the formal rationality of means such as targets or share value.

Alongside the rise of environmental, social and corporate governance (ESG) reporting there has been a growing interest in purpose as a driver of organizational culture and decision making. One example has been the rise of B-Corporations. The B-Corps movement was started by three friends who met at Stanford University. Now, tens of thousands of organizations have applied for a status that involves them openly evaluating their business model and reporting on a range of social and environmental measures.

B

There are also several initiatives that seek to influence consumer behaviour by providing assurances about the employment practices of producers. For example, in 2019 the entrepreneur and philanthropist Julian Richer (supported by business and trade union federations) launched the Good Business Charter, awarded to employers who committed, among other things, to employee wellbeing, representation and fair hours and contracts. Before being forced by public pressure to recant, some high profile business figures showed a lack of concern and compassion in the early stages of COVID.

A   Prisoners work in the kitchen at The Clink restaurant ahead of the lunch service inside Brixton Prison in south London. The Clink serves up to 120 members of the public lunch each day. It is one of four such restaurants run by The Clink charity, which aims to give inmates the skills and qualifications needed to start a new life when they are released.

B   The Volkswagen scandal, in which the company was discovered to have lied and covered up about diesel car emissions, is often cited by those sceptical of corporate claims to be acting responsibly.

But an illustration of an enlightened employer came with a Tweet in September 2020 (as children returned to school after months of COVID lockdown) by James Timpson, the head of a UK chain of repair stores which is committed to training and employing ex-offenders;

'If you find our shops a bit short staffed this week, I'm sorry. We have a colleague benefit where you get an extra day off when your kids have their first day at school, so a number of colleagues are doing a very special job away from the shops.'

Some commentators, including for example Luc Boltanski and and Eve Chiapello, authors of *The New Spirit of Capitalism* (1999), are deeply sceptical of what they see as attempts to replace old-fashioned command and control with a softer, more devolved image of capitalist employment. It is certainly the case that several firms – from Enron to Volkswagen – have had their attempt to present a benign image smashed by major exposés of corporate wrongdoing, which generally involved staff following orders from above.

A

A more radical challenge to both the relationship between ownership and control and the structural conflict of interest between producers and consumers lies in the co-operative movement. The principles of mutuality lying behind co-operatives echo both our prehistoric collectivism and medieval crafts guilds. The modern idea of co-operatives is often traced to the 'Rochdale pioneers' who set up a food co-op in 1844 and published seven principles that continue to be followed by many co-ops today:

1. Voluntary and open membership

2. Democratic member control, with each member having one vote

3. Economic participation by members

4. Autonomy and independence

5. Education, training and information

6. Co-operation among co-operatives

7. Concern for community

The **co-operative movement** is a worldwide movement of producers, workers snd consumers (or a combination of them), working broadly along co-operative principles established in the 19th century.

Although the **Rochdale pioneers**, or the Rochdale Society of Equitable Pioneers, was not the first consumer co-operative, it provided the template on which the co-operative movement grew in Britain and globally, including the Rochdale principles.

A   Banners for co-op women's guilds. Co-operatives offer staff a greater voice and more of stake in the success of a company.
B   Co-operatives have been common among farmers and are sometimes supported by government, as in the case of banana growers in Ivory Coast.
C   Teachers and students help farmers with the cabbage harvest at an agricultural co-operative near Minsk, Belarus.

Notably, there are significant overlaps between these points and the seven RSA / Carnegie good work characteristics.

There is now a wide variety of co-operative forms across the world in sectors ranging from farming and manufacture to banking and consultancy. They include The Mondragon Corporation, a federation of worker co-operatives based in the Basque region of Spain in which, overall, over 80,000 people are employed. Research in 2012 suggested that over a billion people in 96 countries were members of one or more, mainly consumer, co-operatives. By their nature co-ops challenge some of the problematic aspects of work explored in the last chapter. By spreading ownership among all employees, they address the imbalance of power and influence between owners and employees in traditional organizations (Elizabeth Anderson's 'private government'). Producer and consumer co-operatives can also balance the need to compete in the market with adherence to ethical principles and internal democracy. Co-operatives seek to apply the same values to consumption choices as production systems.

B

C

Mindful and ethical consumption is surely essential. Not only does it enable better work and contribute to a more sustainable system but by focusing on quality of life rather than quantity of stuff, it might also help us live in less frenetic ways, less susceptible to social media-induced fears of missing out and more able to resist the allure of easy credit. Sooner or later we must step off the hedonic treadmill.

Despite their growth and popularity, co-operatives are still an exception to conventional forms of ownership in control. Because they do not offer profits to outside investors, they can often have difficulty in attracting capital. Several mutuals, especially in the financial services sector, have been subject to successful campaigns to demutualize led by members seeking the windfall gain from having their shares bought out by conventional investors. These included UK building societies which were targeted in the 1980s and 1990s by 'carpet baggers' who bought shares solely to campaign for demutualization and make a fast return.

A

A   In the 1990s many mutual building societies became targets of speculative 'carpetbaggers', who opened savings accounts in order to obtain a windfall in the event of demutualization

B   The Nigerian stock exchange, October 2015. Because of their commitment to profit-sharing, co-operatives can often find it hard to generate market investment.

Mutuals are owned by, and run for, their members and therefore have no external shareholders and will have an asset lock to ensure the funds of the organization are not dispersed beyond the membership either while it is functioning or if it is wound up.

B

Research suggests that overall co-operatives are more resilient than privately owned enterprises, but they are not perfect. They can be hierarchical and sometimes fall prey to the same commercial and competitive pressures and practices as other organizations. Nevertheless, were co-operative models to expand, perhaps even to become the norm for employers and consumers, it could make a major difference to the way people relate to work and to each other.

There are certain sectors where a growth in co-operatives could be particularly impactful. They could, for example, provide a solution to issues like how to have the benefits of gig work without the dangers of exploitation inherent in privately controlled platforms owned by profit hungry investors. With the importance of relatedness as an intrinsic motivation in mind, another area calling out for the co-operative approach is care.

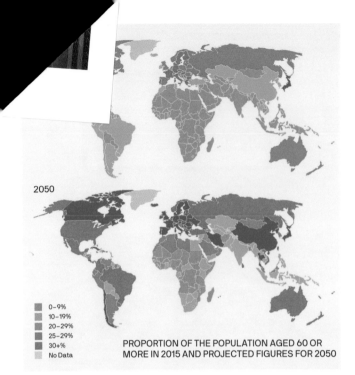

2050

0–9%
10–19%
20–29%
25–29%
30+%
No Data

PROPORTION OF THE POPULATION AGED 60 OR
MORE IN 2015 AND PROJECTED FIGURES FOR 2050

A

IPPR (Institute of Public Policy Research) is the UK's leading left of centre think tank. Its work has been very influential in shaping the policies of Labour and other political parties.

Self-care refers to the deliberate steps taken by an individual to sustain their own physical and mental wellbeing. Self-care has become a particularly important part of strategies to manage chronic medical conditions.

Populations are ageing across the world and care will continue to grow as a share of the labour market. As we saw in chapter 1, care is a form of work which has moved from being largely an unpaid duty flowing from our way of life to being widely commoditized. But, as the COVID-19 crisis grimly illustrated, even in wealthy countries, many care systems are in a parlous state.

A 2018 study by the think tank IPPR (Institute of Public Policy Research), highlighting poor pay and conditions in the sector, predicted a shortfall of 400,000 social care workers in the UK by 2028. Feminist writers such as Eva Feder Kittay and Madeleine Bunting have argued that care's unjustifiably low status and remuneration levels can only be fully understood in terms of patriarchal domination and definitions of social value.

Given the necessity of care and the vulnerability of many of those receiving it, the pursuit of profit as a primary goal is highly problematic.

A   Maps showing the growing proportion of older people over the first half of the 21st century. The health and care workforce is bound to grow to meet this demand.

B   An elderly woman enjoys the cherry blossoms in full bloom with the help of her carer who pushes her wheelchair in Nakano, Tokyo. Many more people could work in care: a Health Foundation report published in late 2019 found the number of vacancies for social care workers in England alone running at 110,000.

The Buurtzorg example shows the best care systems achieve an effective combination of self-care, informal unpaid care and professional support. But if care is being provided privately, voluntary efforts can be exploited to boost profit margins. Similarly, in bureaucratic public systems with tight criteria for eligibility, there is an incentive for people to emphasize their dependency. Co-operatives, with workers, patients and carers all having a stake in the organization's success have a better opportunity to combine different types of work; paid formal care on the one hand with informal familial care and wider community support on the other.

B

New organizational forms, industrial democracy and co-operatives all offer scope for ways of working which overcome some of the aspects of work which make it onerous and alienating. Currently these models are at the margins but with support from policy makers and continued development, they could augur a new era in which work feels more continuous with our other values and life aspirations.

The third of Deci and Ryan's intrinsic motivations – competence – offers another important angle on fulfilling work. Why are we good at some things and not others? For many of us the route we took in education and our career was down to contingent factors; family expectations, a teacher who inspired us, a short-term job that became permanent. At retirement many people choose to develop some of the many skills or interests they had to ignore during their working lives. But for those suffering poverty or failing health this opportunity is limited.

A

B

A   A group of graduates at Dhaka University, Bangladesh, expressing their delight, 2018. The expansion of higher edcuation has been a major global trend over recent decades.

B   A woman celebrates her graduation in San Jose, California. Advanced education is rightly seen as route to social mobility and employment, but it can also lead us to abandon other interests and enthusiasms.

C   A class at a study centre in Seoul, South Korea, 2013. In Seoul's *Goshichon*, literally 'Exam Village', about 20,000 students study all week preparing for the civil service exams or the bar exam. Over recent decades in many school systems the focus has been on academic standards and 'teaching to the test'. Other subjects, particularly related to creativity, have been marginalized.

As a reflection of how we think of work, education systems tend to be oriented to the needs of our economy and to our role in that economy. In Warren Buffet's grimly instrumental words, often quoted by education ministers, 'the more you learn, the more you earn'.

If our society and our view of useful work were based on the fulfilment of human potential, we would want schools to have different priorities. On the one hand, the curriculum would be very broad; seeking to give every child a wide range of experiences and challenges. On the other, schools would be judged by their ability to discover every child's greatest aptitudes and enthusiasm wherever they may lie.

Employability is the capacity of someone to get a job, succeed in a job and to be able to get another job if they need to. Increasingly employers see employability as being about 'soft skills' such as team work, creativity and communication.

Yet in many countries, policy has gone in the opposite direction. An unerring focus on standards and narrow ideas of employability has led to less time for art, culture and sport, particularly in working-class schools where children have fewer opportunities at home.

Recall the view of Matthew Crawford – the American professor who combines being a public philosopher with running a motor bike repair shop; learning to work with resistant materials like wood or metal can ground and inspire people in ways the virtual world of screens and software never could. It is in craft and engagement with the natural world that we may be most likely to attain Mihaly Csikszentmihalyi's state of 'flow'. Yet, apart from some very basic activities in primary school, it is now easy for children to go through their whole education without having any opportunity to experience, let alone develop, manual skills or an appreciation of craft.

What makes this more perverse is the impact technology is likely to have on our economy and lives. This impact has likely been accelerated by COVID-19. Early in the crisis the economist and former business leader Adair Turner wrote an article entitled 'robots don't get sick' and evidence a few months into the crisis pointed to an acceleration in take up of technology by small and medium sized firms. A more automated future – in which AI and robotics have transformed the labour market – is one in which there will be a greater premium on human creativity. As the late Sir Ken Robinson (1950–2020), whose inspirational speeches on education have been viewed tens of millions of times, said, 'creativity now is as important in education as literacy and we should treat it with the same status.'

Nor is this only about schools or colleges. Many people discover their true calling later in life. A society that understands work to be about self-expression and fulfilment would take for granted that formal and informal learning should continue throughout our lives. Every job should include structured learning opportunities. This is an essential way of responding in the short and medium term to the disruption likely to be caused by technology and, in the longer term, preparing for a future in which paid employment may be a smaller part of our lives.

c

A This graph, showing the projected fastest disappearing jobs in the US, shows how technology can have a severe impact on specific roles.

B Employees in 2021 on the production line at a silicon wafer workshop in Nantong, Jiangsu Province of China, and operating a tool in a 'clean room' in Dresden, Germany. Skilled jobs such as these pay well but will not replace the jobs made redundant by technology.

Conversations about the future of work too often begin with some form of the question 'how must society adapt to techno-logical change?' Technological determinism, along with the ruthless ways tech business giants are using their know-how and power, is one of the reasons many industrialized countries exhibit high levels of pessimism. If, instead, we looked at the future from the perspective of human thriving our view might be very different.

A

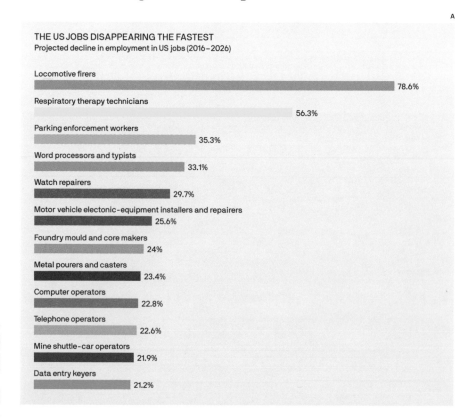

THE US JOBS DISAPPEARING THE FASTEST
Projected decline in employment in US jobs (2016–2026)

Locomotive firers — 78.6%

Respiratory therapy technicians — 56.3%

Parking enforcement workers — 35.3%

Word processors and typists — 33.1%

Watch repairers — 29.7%

Motor vehicle electonic-equipment installers and repairers — 25.6%

Foundry mould and core makers — 24%

Metal pourers and casters — 23.4%

Computer operators — 22.8%

Telephone operators — 22.6%

Mine shuttle-car operators — 21.9%

Data entry keyers — 21.2%

Technological determinism is the view that the key stages of human history and future possibilities are the direct result of changes in the development and take-up of technology.

The **World Economic Forum** is an independent international organization committed to 'improving the world' through engaging senior figures in business and politics and thought leadership.

The **fourth industrial revolution** is the term applied by a number of writers and organizations to emerging technology, particularly Artificial Intelligence and robotics and its impact on the economy and society.

B

Throughout history – from the first farming tools to the combine harvester, from the printing press to the microprocessor – technological change has shaped our lives and our work. This has led to a largely materialist view of what shapes work. But depending on how we think about work and who controls it, the same technology can be liberating or enslaving.

As we embark on what many – including the World Economic Forum – are calling the fourth industrial revolution how we think about work is vital. We have a choice.

Conclusion

A

A   A street cleaner in deserted
    Podgorica, Montenegro, March
    2020. COVID has changed the
    way we work more radically
    and quickly than anything
    in peacetime. It offers the
    chance for a rethink about
    what work is for.
B   A New York based woman
    working at home in casual
    clothes. Like many people she
    reports that the pandemic has
    impacted not just her work but
    her consumption patterns too.
    Will new habits remain after
    the pandemic?

Human beings have worked to survive, they have worked because they were forced to, worked because it was the place ordained for them by God, worked to earn and consume. There have been times when work did not exist separate from day-to-day living, times when society's elites have scorned work as beneath them, times when the work you did was likely to define your affiliations and beliefs, times when work was simply a means to an end. Knowing how much has changed should open our eyes to new possibilities. We should aspire to a new era of work.

The experience of COVID-19 has led us to ask deeper questions about our lives and our societies. Despite the death, fear and disruption caused by the pandemic and its aftermath, opinion surveys show most people do not want to go back to how things were before.

Work-life balance relates both to people's experience of managing their lives inside and outside work and also to a range of measures, such as flexible working hours and working from home, which are intended to help people manage.

The focus on key workers led to people being more aware and more critical of the gap between the social value of work and the material rewards and status it generates. For many people various levels of lockdown meant big changes in work. Those who could, worked from home, and some said they wanted to carry on even when the immediate danger of infection had passed.

It may be that more people can achieve a better work-life balance. But the very idea of 'balancing' work and life underlines a separation between how we earn an income and what matters to us. A more radical goal is to blur the boundaries between work for earning, for living and for thriving. If we expected to find our work enjoyable and meaningful, if we saw being an active citizen in our locality and community as a universal expectation, if we treated all forms of care as an essential and highly valued human activity then perhaps we could aim not for balance but 'work life integration'.

B

Climate emergency is a phrase the environmental movement has successfully brought into public debate as a means of highlighting the urgent and profound nature of the challenge of tacking climate change.

Western Enlightenment is a term applied to ideas and social innovations that arose in Western Europe in the 18th and early 19th century; amongst which the ideals of autonomy, universalism and progress through scientific and technological discovery were central.

The big challenges that existed before the pandemic are still there and, if anything, even more acute. How do we tackle inequality and the anger and alienation it has caused? How do we respond to the ever-worsening climate emergency? How do we ensure that the immense opportunities of science and technology are used for the benefit of people and the planet, not simply to add to the power of autocrats and billionaires? How does the liberal democratic project renew itself in the face of its critics, restoring the belief in progress that has been at its heart since its origins in the Western Enlightenment?

A

A Extinction Rebellion (XR) protesters in London in 2019. XR has used high profile acts of civil disobedience to draw attention to the climate emergency.

B XR protestors in Paris and London, in October and April 2019, believe this is a time to make fundamental choices about our future. The challenges we faced before the pandemic, including climate change, poverty and inequality, will be even more pressing after it has passed.

The simple idea that work should be a source of pleasure, fulfilment and growth for all could be the inspiration we need. The first step is a leap of imagination. The environmental economist Tim Jackson memorably described the need to abandon a model of consumerism in which 'people are persuaded to spend money we don't have, on things we don't need, to create impressions that won't last, on people we don't care about.' We need to free ourselves from the idea that we have no choice but to spend our lives doing things we would rather not do, for reasons we did not choose, for people who do not have our best interests at heart. The cause of good work for all could be part of a broader qualitative shift in our world view and lifestyles, one that is essential if we are to build a truly sustainable economy.

B

A

Palliative care is medical and other interventions which seek to minimize unnecessary suffering for those with a terminal health condition, often provided in hospices.

The **World Health Organization (WHO)** is the agency of the United Nations responsible for international public health. The WHO came to greater prominence in the COVID pandemic but was also attacked, including by Donald Trump who withdrew US funding.

The Australian writer Bronnie Ware was for several years a palliative care nurse looking after people in the final weeks of their lives. In 2012 she wrote a blog which quickly became viral and was subsequently the basis of a book. Ware described the five most frequent regrets expressed by people at the very end of their lives. Two were 'I wish I had stayed in touch with my friends' and 'I wish I'd had the courage to express my feelings'. These are relevant to work but the other three are even more striking:

'I wish I'd had the courage to live a life true to myself not the life others expected of me.'

'I wish I had let myself be happier.'

'I wish I hadn't worked so hard.'

In many parts of society there are signs of a wellbeing crisis. The World Health Organization (WHO) has reported that globally one in five adolescents experience a serious mental health issue in any given year. Compared to the world's poorest people, citizens of developed economies have freedom but many of the choices we make collectively and as individuals make us unnecessarily unhappy. A certain level of inequality is inevitable in a free society but in most nations, excessive differences in income, wealth and status make societies more divided and people more insecure. The marketing-led portrayal of consumption as the best way to express our individuality drives us to unsustainable, futile and sometimes self-destructive behaviour. The online world, largely designed to maximize profits, can foster self-obsession, addiction, misinformation and polarization.

The way that many people feel trapped in their jobs reflects and reinforces a wider sense of powerlessness in the face of the gap between how life is and how it would be if we were to thrive and to build a better world for future generations. To break out we need an idea that is visionary but concrete, transformative but attainable. An idea that can turn the potential of technology from a threat to a promise. Why can't that idea be a working life that is built around who we are, what we need and what we are capable of?

Yes, we need to work. The question is: 'Does it need to feel like work?'

B

Further Reading

Anderson, Elizabeth, *Private Government: How Employers Rule Our Lives (And Why We Don't Talk About It)* (Princeton, NJ: Princeton University Press, 2017)

Arendt, Hannah, *The Human Condition* (Chicago, IL: University of Chicago Press, 1958)

Arntz, Melanie, Gregory, Terry and Zierahn, Ulrich, *The Risk of Automation for Jobs in OECD Countries: A Comparative Analysis,* (Paris: OECD, 2016)

Balaram, Brhmie and Wallace-Stephens, Fabian, *Seven Portraits of Economic security and Modern Work in the UK* (London: RSA, 2018)

Bastani, Aaron, *Fully Automated Luxury Communism* (London; New York, NY: Verso, 2019)

Bell, Daniel, *The Cultural Contradictions of Capitalism*, 20th anniversary edition (New York, NY: Basic Books, 1996)

Boltanski, L. and Chiapello, E., *The New Spirit of Capitalism* (Paris: Gallimard, 1999)

Brickman, Philip and Campbell, Donald T., 'Hedonic relativism and planning the good society' in Mortimer H. Appley, ed., *Adaptation-level Theory: A Symposium* (New York, NY: Academic Press, 1971) pp. 287–302

Bunting, Madeleine, *Labours of Love: The Crisis of Care* (London: Granta Books, 2020)

Cockshott, Paul, *How the World Works: The Story of Human Labour from Prehistory to the Modern Day* (New York, NY: Monthly Review Press, 2019)

Crawford, Matthew B., *The Case for Working With Your Hands: Or Why Office Work is Bad for Us and Fixing Things Feels Good* (London: Viking, 2009)

Crawford, Matthew B., *Shop Class as Soulcraft* (New York, NY: Penguin, 2009)

Csikszentmihalyi, Mihaly, *Flow: the Psychology of Optimal Experience* (London; New York, NY: HarperCollins, 2009)

Donkin, Richard, *The History of Work* (London: Palgrave Macmillan, 2010)

Frey, Carl B. and Osborne, Michael A., 'The Future of Employment and How Susceptivle are Jobs to Computerization', *Technological Forecasting and Social Change,* Volume 114, 2017, pp. 254-28

Giddens, Anthony, *Capitalism and Modern Social Theory: An Analysis of the Writings of Marx, Durkheim and Max Weber* (Cambridge: Cambridge University Press, 1971)

Graeber, David, *Bullshit Jobs: A Theory* (New York, NY: Simon and Schuster, 2018)

Inglehart, Ronald, *Culture Shift in Advanced Industrial Society* (Princeton, NJ: Princeton University Press, 1990)

Irvine, Gail, White, Douglas and Diffley, Mark, *Measuring Good Work: The Final Report of the Measuring Job Quality Working Group* (Dunfermline : Carnegie UK Trust, 2018)

Keynes, John Maynard, 'Economic Possibilities for our Grandchildren' in *Essays in Persuasion* (New York, NY: Harcourt Brace, 1932), pp. 358-73

Kittay, Eva Feder and Feder, Ellen K., *The Subject of Care: Feminist Perspectives on Dependency* (Lanham, MD: Rowman and Littlefield, 2002)

Komlosy, Andrea, *Work: The Last Thousand Years* (London; New York, NY: Verso, 2018)

Laloux, Frederic, *Reinventing Organizations: A Guide to Creating Organizations Inspired by the Next Stage of Human Consciousness* (Brussels: Nelson Parker, 2014)

Mayo, Ed, *A Short History of Co-Operation and Mutuality* (Manchester: Co-operatives UK, 2017)

Pink, Daniel H., *To Sell is Human: The Surprising Truth About Persuading, Convincing, and Influencing Others* (New York, NY: Riverhead Books, 2012)

Polanyi, Karl, *The Great Transformation: The Political and Economic Origins of Our Time* (Boston, MA: Beacon, 1944)

Robinson, Ken, *The Element: How Finding Your Passion Changes Everything* (London: Penguin, 2009)

Sahlins, M. 'Notes on the Original Affluent Society' in Richard B. Lee and Irene DeVore, *Man the Hunter: The First Intensive Survey of a Single, Crucial Stage of Human Development* (New York, NY: Aldine Publishing Company, 1968) pp. 85–89

Siméon, Ophélie, *Robert Owen's Experiment at New Lanark: From Paternalism to Socialism* (London: Palgrave Macmillan, 2017)

Srnicek, Nick and Williams, Alex, *Inventing the Future: Post-Capitalism and a World Without Work* (London: Verso, 2016)

Tawney, R. H., *Religion and the Rise of Capitalism* (London: John Murray, 1926)

Taylor, Frederick Winslow, *The Principles of Scientific Management* (New York, NY; London: Harper & Brothers, 1911)

Taylor, Matthew, *Good work; The Taylor Review of Modern Working Practices* (London: HMSO, 2017)

Turner, Adair, 'Robots Don't Get Sick: Accelerated Automation' in the Post-Covid World', *Montrose Journal*, 2020

Veblen, Thorstein, *The Theory of the Leisure Class: An Economic Study of Institutions,* (New York, NY: Macmillan, 1899)

Vermeer, Astrid and Wenting, Ben, *Self-Management: How Does it Work?* (Houten : Bohn Stafleu van Loghum, 2018)

Wallace-Stephens, Fabian, *Economic Insecurity: The Case for a Twenty-first Century Safety Net* (London: RSA, 2019)

Ware, Bonnie, *The Top Five Regrets of Dying: A Life Transformed by the Dearly Departing* (London: Hay House, 2011)

Weber, Max, *The Protestant Ethic and the Spirit of Capitalism,* trans. Talcott Parsons (London : George Allen & Unwin Ltd., 1930)

Picture Credits

Every effort has been made to locate and credit copyright holders of the material reproduced in this book. The author and publisher apologize for any omissions or errors, which can be corrected in future editions.

a = above, b = below,
c = centre, l = left, r = right

67a Photoquest/
Getty Images
67b Hulton Archive/
Getty Images
68l Peter Turnley/Corbis/
VCG via Getty Image
68r Vittoriano Rastelli/
Corbis via Getty Images
69 John Dominis/The LIFE
Picture Collection
via Getty Images
70l Incamerastock/
Alamy Stock Photo
70r Library of Congress,
Washington D.C.
71 Etsy
72a Tom Nicholson/LNP/
Shutterstock
72b Michele Lapini/
Getty Images
73 Patrick T. Fallon/
Bloomberg via
Getty Images
74–5 ©Peter Marlow/
Magnum Photos
76 ©Steve McCurry/
Magnum Photos
77a Jordi Boixareu/ZUMA
Wire/Shutterstock
77b ©Susan Meiselas/
Magnum Photos
78 Thames & Hudson
79 S. M. Swenson/
Getty Images
80 TUC Library Collections
at London Metropolitan
University
81a Manuel Dorati/
NurPhoto via
Getty Images
81b Carsten Koall/
Getty Images
82 Sueddeutsche
Zeitung Photo/
Alamy Stock Photo
83a Ahn Young-joon/
AP/Shutterstock
83b Michael Nagle/
Bloomberg
via Getty Images
84l Bettmann/Getty Images
84r Dave Hogan/
Getty Images
85 PA Images/Alamy
Stock Photo
86 Reuters/Alamy
Stock Photo
87a Muhammad Fadli/
Bloomberg
via Getty Images
87b StockStudio Aerials
88l, c KK Awards
88r The Music Stand

89a Craig Warga/Bloomberg
via Getty Images
89b Justin Sullivan/
Getty Images
90 Thames & Hudson
91 Allan Cash Picture
Library/Alamy
Stock Photo
92 Cris Faga/NurPhoto
via Getty Images
93a Miguel Medina/AFP
via Getty Images
93b Hector Retamal/AFP
via Getty Images
94 Instagram
95l, c Ed Endicott/
Alamy Stock Photo
95r Steve Cukrov/
Alamy Stock Photo
96 AA Film Archive/
Alamy Stock Photo
97al John Meyer/
Alamy Stock Photo
97ar Douglas Lander/
Alamy Stock Photo
97bl DPD ImageStock/
Alamy Stock Photo
97br Brendon Thorne/
Bloomberg via
Getty Images
98–9 Ruhani Kaur/Bloomberg
via Getty Images
100 Thames & Hudson
101 Jesus Merida/Sopa
Images/LightRocket
via Getty Images
102 Jonathan Wong/South
China Morning Post
via Getty Images
103a Zuma Press, Inc./
Alamy Stock Photo
103b Shoko Takayasu/
Bloomberg via
Getty Images
104 Thames & Hudson
106a Yasuyoshi Chiba/
AFP via Getty Images
106b Drew Angerer/Getty
Images
107a Stephane De Sakutin/
AFP via Getty Images
107b Kirill Kukhmar/TASS
via Getty Images
108 Merlyn Severn/Picture
Post/IPC Magazines/
Hulton Archive/
Getty Images
109 Thames & Hudson
110 ©Olivia Arthur/
Magnum Photos
111a Scott Strazzante/San
Francisco Chronicle
via Getty Images

111b Neil Hall/EPA-EFE/
Shutterstock
112 Thames & Hudson
113 B Corp
114 Justin Tallis/AFP
via Getty Images
115 Justin Metz © 2016
116l, r North Lanarkshire
Museums, 1987-24-1,
1987-24-4
117l Legnan Koula/EPA-EFE/
Shutterstock
117r Sergey Balay/AFP
via Getty Images
118 David Soulsby/
Alamy Stock Photo
119a George Osodi/Bloomberg
via Getty Images
119b Pius Utomi Ekpei/
AFP via Getty Images
120 UNDESA Population
division
121 Yusuke Harada/NurPhoto
via Getty Images
122a Zakir Hossain
Chowdhury/NurPhoto
via Getty Images
122b Randy Vazquez/Bay
Digital First Media/
Mercury News via
Getty Images
123 ©Sim Chi Yin/
Magnum Photos
124a Yegor Aleyev/TASS
via Getty Images
124b Gregory Rec/Portland
Press Herald via
Getty Images
125 Jonathan Raa/NurPhoto
via Getty Images
126 Thames & Hudson
127a Xu Congjun/VCG
via Getty Images
127b Liesa Johannssen-
Koppitz/Bloomberg
via Getty Images
128–9 ©Carolyn Drake/
Magnum Photos
130 Milos Vujovic/Anadolu
Agency via Getty Images
131 Alejandra Villa Loarca/
Newsday RM via
Getty Images
132l, r ©Martin Parr/
Magnum Photos
133l ©Richard Kalvar/
Magnum Photos
133r Mike Kemp/In Pictures
via Getty Images Images
134 Nareshkumar Shaganti/
Alamy Stock Photo
135 Ahn Young-joon/
AP/Shutterstock

Index

Acknowledgments:
I would like to thank Jane Laing and the team
at Thames & Hudson. As series editor of The Big
Ideas, I'm delighted that my book now joins the
other 13 titles. Appropriately perhaps for a book
about new ways of working, this one was written
entirely during lockdown. I am grateful to the RSA
for giving me the time to complete the book and
to Ruth for reading, improving and even helping
me identify pictures and captions.

First published in the United Kingdom in 2021
by Thames & Hudson Ltd, 181A High Holborn,
London WC1V 7QX

First published in the United States of America
in 2021 by Thames & Hudson Inc., 500 Fifth Avenue,
New York, New York 10110

Do We Have To Work? © 2021
Thames & Hudson Ltd, London

Text © 2021 Matthew Taylor

For image copyright information, see pp. 138–39

British Library Cataloguing-in-Publication Data
A catalogue record for this book is available from
the British Library

Library of Congress Control Number 2021934173

ISBN 978-0-500-29622-6

Printed and bound in Slovenia by DZS Grafik

MIX
Paper from
responsible sources
FSC® C112556

Be the first to know about our new releases,
exclusive content and author events by visiting
thamesandhudson.com
thamesandhudsonusa.com
thamesandhudson.com.au